THE TRANS–PACIFIC PARTNERSHIP:
PROSPECTS FOR GREATER U.S. TRADE

HEARING

BEFORE THE

SUBCOMMITTEE ON ASIA AND THE PACIFIC

OF THE

COMMITTEE ON FOREIGN AFFAIRS
HOUSE OF REPRESENTATIVES

ONE HUNDRED FOURTEENTH CONGRESS

FIRST SESSION

MARCH 4, 2015

Serial No. 114–14

Printed for the use of the Committee on Foreign Affairs

Available via the World Wide Web: http://www.foreignaffairs.house.gov/ or
http://www.gpo.gov/fdsys/

U.S. GOVERNMENT PUBLISHING OFFICE

93–670PDF   WASHINGTON : 2015

For sale by the Superintendent of Documents, U.S. Government Publishing Office
Internet: bookstore.gpo.gov   Phone: toll free (866) 512–1800; DC area (202) 512–1800
Fax: (202) 512–2104   Mail: Stop IDCC, Washington, DC 20402–0001

CONTENTS

Page

WITNESSES

Claude Barfield, Ph.D., resident scholar, American Enterprise Institute 4
Ms. Tami Overby, senior vice president for Asia, U.S. Chamber of Commerce . 21
Mr. Scott Miller, senior adviser and William M. Scholl Chair in International
Business, Center for Strategic and International Studies 33
Ms. Celeste Drake, trade and globalization policy specialist, The American
Federation of Labor and Congress of Industrial Organizations 40

LETTERS, STATEMENTS, ETC., SUBMITTED FOR THE HEARING

Claude Barfield, Ph.D.: Prepared statement 7
Ms. Tami Overby: Prepared statement 23
Mr. Scott Miller: Prepared statement 35
Ms. Celeste Drake: Prepared statement 42

APPENDIX

Hearing notice.. 80
Hearing minutes.. 81
The Honorable Gerald E. Connolly, a Representative in Congress from the
Commonwealth of Virginia: Prepared statement 82
The Honorable Tom Marino, a Representative in Congress from the Common-
wealth of Pennsylvania: Questions submitted to the witnesses for the
record 84

THE TRANS–PACIFIC PARTNERSHIP: PROSPECTS FOR GREATER U.S. TRADE

WEDNESDAY, MARCH 4, 2015

House of Representatives,
Subcommittee on Asia and the Pacific,
Committee on Foreign Affairs,
Washington, DC.

The committee met, pursuant to notice, at 3 o'clock p.m., in room 2172 Rayburn House Office Building, Hon. Matt Salmon (chairman of the committee) presiding.

Mr. SALMON. The hearing will come to order. I would like to thank the witnesses for participating in what promises to be a lively hearing. I look forward to hearing from you about our trade opportunities in Asia. And I want to thank Ranking Member Sherman. We approach trade quite differently, but I am looking forward to having this debate and having a great group of testimonies from the members of the panel.

The scale of our economic ties with Asia is vast. Three of seven of our top trading partners are in Asia. Three of our top six holders of U.S. Treasury bonds are in Asia, where their combined ownership exceeds $2.5 trillion. Trade, especially U.S. economic and trade policy in the Asia Pacific will be one of the major issues this Congress will deliberate. Increased U.S. presence in the region through the Trans-Pacific Partnership would greatly improve the American economy as well as provide considerable diplomatic and strategic benefits.

Let me start off by saying we live in a globalized world. That has already happened. Nothing is going to change that whether anybody here likes it or not. It is only right for the United States to take advantage of the opportunities that globalization can afford us, especially as it can improve the livelihoods of Americans and improve trade and labor conditions abroad. Excluding ourselves from a monumental trade agreement that has clearly distinguished itself from previous FTAs would be unproductive and detrimental to our interests in Asia. The TPP would provide comprehensive and high standard guidelines for trade and commerce in the Asia Pacific. A robust and comprehensive TPP has the potential to improve our economy and provide consistency and stability in Asia.

When Congress passes TPP, the world will know we are dedicated to economic prosperity through the facilitation of strong and inclusive rules-based, market-oriented economic growth. While the details of the trade agreement are still not public, I am confident that TPP will address issues such as preventing state-owned enter-

(1)

prises from having an unfair advantage in a market, or setting clear rules of origin, or constructing safeguards to protect intellectual property. I am also confident that TPP will foster job creation by incentivizing industry to invest in domestic production and manufacturing.

Opponents of free trade will say our country will be flooded with low cost imports. It is important to note the United States already has relatively low tariffs and minimal other trade barriers, with 70 percent of our imports already duty free.

We should not be worried about imports flooding our market after TPP has passed. Instead, TPP will help lower trade barriers for U.S. manufacturers and companies that are seeking access to other countries, providing U.S. trade and investment opportunities with other countries.

If the United States does not participate in a comprehensive multilateral agreement in Asia, we may lose out on opportunities for growth and influence in the region. China is leading the way in pushing for an alternative regional economic and trade agreement called the Regional Comprehensive Economic Partnership, or RCEP, which excludes the United States. Reports have indicated that negotiations may focus on broad issues and avoid sensitive areas, so it will likely to be a lower standard trade agreement. Additionally, the agreement would facilitate intra-RCEP trade by lowering tariffs among participating countries, but it would the exclude the United States from those trade benefits.

As China takes the lead in proposing alternative economic futures for Asia at the exclusion of the United States, the TPP would reassert our presence in the region. Through TPP, we would be able to shape rules and introduce U.S. practices to countries like Vietnam to improve conditions for human rights and labor practices, or provide environmental protection and intellectual property rights protection clauses. We would not see those types of provisions in a China-led trade agreement, I can assure you.

China can allege that the United States is rebalancing to Asia purely to achieve military outcomes, but the successful negotiation and implementation of a TPP agreement will counter Beijing's notions that we are only focused on the security rebalance to Asia as well as reassure allies and our friends in the region that we are a reliable economic partner. After all, the United States has been, and will continue to be a Pacific power.

I look forward to hearing our distinguished witnesses this morning and hope they will be able to address how the TPP would set guidelines that would improve our economic strength both at home and abroad and tell us what steps are necessary for a successful outcome.

I now yield to Mr. Sherman, the ranking member of the subcommittee, for his opening remarks, and then we will move quickly to questions because we have a few members that have to get to airplanes. Thank you, Mr. Sherman.

Mr. SHERMAN. Mr. Chairman, we are having this hearing as many of our colleagues are leaving. Just because all the seats are not filled does not mean that this matter is not of critical importance.

A look at the economics of the various trade deals leaves a stark picture. We were told that giving most favored nation status permanently to China would increase our trade deficit by $1 billion. That estimate was off by over 30,000 percent. We were told that the Korea deal would reduce our trade deficit. It increases it. And now we can't even find an economist who says that this deal will reduce our trade deficit or increase jobs, so instead they are telling us that somehow this increases national income. But of course not the income of those who need jobs.

The economic case for this agreement is so incredibly weak that even with the vast majority of economists already on the payroll of those who are pushing it they can't make an economic case. And so we are given other reasons. We are told isn't it wonderful to have a deal with the rules that came from the United States? And it is true that many of the approaches behind this agreement were written on Wall Street.

That we should take pride in such rules is like turning to citizens from Madrid and saying take pride in the Spanish flu, because these rules have decimated millions and millions of American middle class families. We need fair trade, not what is called free trade.

And the choice is not between the status quo and digging in further. But instead we have the lowest tariffs; many of them we can raise in an effort to force countries to adopt fair trade, results-oriented trade agreements. When you are in a hole, and we have the biggest trade deficit hole imaginable, it is time to stop digging.

Then we are told, oh well, yes, it is a terrible economic deal, but think of how it helps us geopolitically against China. No, this is a deal that helps China. First, look at the rules of origin in the Korea agreement, and what we would expect to see is rules of origin here. Goods that are 65 percent admitted made in China, which means they may be 70, 80, 90 percent made in China, they get a "Made in Korea" tag put on them that is the value added in Korea; they come into our country duty free and we get no benefits, no access to the Chinese market. This is a free trade agreement on steroids with China one way.

Then the agreement says nothing about currency manipulation, so it enshrines the Chinese idea that currency manipulation is just fine. And those who violate the law by refusing to designate China as a currency manipulator come up with a PowerPoint presentation to show me that China is cheating but they are cheating less so let us not do anything about that. Folks, imagine trying that on your spouse. Honey, I am cheating less. Here is my PowerPoint demonstration, mistresses per month sharply declining. Wouldn't work. Cheating less is not a good way to argue that we should continue this process. So the idea that we can give away jobs and that proves how geopolitically strong we are is rather crazy.

And finally we look at statistics. Every time a statistic points in the direction this costs jobs, I hear, they hire a dozen economists to tell me, well that statistic, you don't like that statistic. It has a flaw. What you also see is that if a deal increases our imports by 2 billion and increases our exports by 1 billion, we are told it is a great deal because it is 3 billion more in trade. Or told it is a great deal because it is $1 billion more in exports. Nobody—I mean I am a CPA. I don't expect everybody to be CPA, but even in elementary school you learn how to add but you also learn how to subtract. And that fact is that if exports help, imports have the opposite effect.

Finally, Secretary Kerry in this room said that this deal will not be a race to the bottom. Then why are we including Vietnam? Thirty cents an hour, that is the bottom. And we are told, well this deal will get us free access to their markets. Vietnam has no freedom and has no markets. And so finally Secretary Kerry says, oh, but we will have labor standards in this agreement. I will want to hear from our witnesses whether they would sell a life insurance policy to someone trying to exercise labor rights in Vietnam. And if so, I am going to make sure that they are never allowed to work for an insurance company or an insurance regulator.

I yield back.

Mr. SALMON. Thank you, Mr. Sherman.

We have a very distinguished panel of four experts today, and we are just thrilled that you could be here. Thank you, and thank you for your patience.

Dr. Claude Barfield is a resident scholar at the American Enterprise Institute. Dr. Barfield covers trade, intellectual property and technology policy, and was previously a consultant for the Office of the U.S. Trade Representative.

Ms. Tami Overby currently serves as Senior Vice President for Asia at the U.S. Chamber of Commerce. She is also the president of U.S-Korea Business Council and has spent decades living in Asia. Thank you.

Mr. Scott Miller is a senior advisor at the Center for Strategic and International Studies. He holds the Center's William M. Scholl Chair in International Business and previously served in roles with the U.S. Trade Representative and Department of State. Thank you, Mr. Miller.

And Ms. Celeste Drake is the Trade and Globalization Policy Specialist at the American Federation of Labor and Congress of Industrial Organizations. Ms. Drake, a lawyer, previously served on congressional staff and as a judicial clerk. Thank you, Ms. Drake.

And we are going to start with you, Dr. Barfield, and then we will move to my right, to your left, and that is not a political spectrum or anything like that necessarily. But we are really appreciative to have you here. You all understand the lighting system. When it goes amber you have a minute left. We are going to try to stick to those times because we would like to get as many questions as we have, and we have a couple of members who are trying to beat the snowstorm. So thank you very much, Dr. Barfield.

STATEMENT OF CLAUDE BARFIELD, PH.D., RESIDENT SCHOLAR, AMERICAN ENTERPRISE INSTITUTE

Mr. BARFIELD. Thank you very much, Mr. Chairman, and thank you very much for inviting me. I will be happy to answer some of your and Mr. Sherman's questions on the economic side, but because in talking with the staff and because this is the foreign relation committee and not the Ways and Means Committee my testimony is largely on the geostrategic implications of the Trans-Pacific Partnership and other regional agreements.

And I will be very brief. And I want to start with a quotation from Thomas Schelling, a Nobel prize winner of a couple of decades ago, who said that the stakes of U.S. trade policy have always reached beyond the economic realm. Trade is what most international relations are about. For that reason, trade policy is national security policy.

The point in my longer testimony that I try to make is summed up in this kind of theme. Whatever Mr. Schelling thought about trade policy and economic policy, trade policy really stands at the intersection between what one might say is the high diplomatic and security policy, our national interests in that regard whether it is in terms of an individual other nation or a region and domestic politics.

How will these trade agreements affect our workers, our businesses? And that juxtaposition is something that Presidents since the late 1980s when the United States moved away from just having a trade policy that was with the GATT, and then ultimately the WTO, to trade policies that really affected individual nations and now the regions.

And so in the 1980s and through the Obama administration, when the Obama administration is trying to decide who we will have a trade agreement with and for what reasons, yes, the Trade Representative is there, but so is representatives from the Secretary of Defense, the Secretary of Commerce, from EPA, from other cabinets and other sub-cabinet representatives. The point is that this affects interests that are beyond just our economic interest.

And this goes back just—and I will briefly, quickly come up to the Obama administration—I mean this started particularly with what we are looking at today with the TPP in terms of Asia with the Secretary of State James Baker under the first George Bush who reacted to a proposal by Japan and Malaysia to have an intra-Asian regional agreement by saying famously that the United States does not intend to allow a line to be drawn down the middle of the Pacific with us on one side of it and the nations of Asia on the other.

And you move forward from the Bush administration to the Clinton administration where with NAFTA, with APEC, with the Free Trade of the Americas you had a strong push also to push democratic values, changing political institutions as well as the economic underpinning. With the Bush administration and the post-9/11 period, trade policy became a part of the white Defense paper in 2003. So you have had across different administrations this connection between geostrategic policy on the one hand and the trade policy on the other.

Let me just briefly talk about the Obama administration because it is the most fascinating, I think, example. Famously, Mr. Obama came into office saying that he would have opposed NAFTA. He did not agree with the Bush trade agreements that had been negotiated after 2001. And yet within several years, the President himself and his administration turned around. Part of that admittedly, the first year they were dealing with an economic crisis, part of that was economic.

The President's advisors kept pushing him saying that trade and certainly exports and more trade agreements will really help our economy as a plus to what we are doing domestically. But the other thing that occurred was that in the Pacific area the diplomatic and security situation was deteriorating. It was when Mr. Obama came to office that you began to have this increased activity of North Korea, the launching of missiles across the East and South China Sea, of threatening Japan, and at the same time that China changed from this so-called peaceful development to a much more vigorous and assertive and belligerent policy.

So it was actually cutting across our relations with some of our, and as we see even today with some of our chief allies—with the Japanese, with the Philippines, with even Vietnam, Malaysia and Indonesia. So that really what the administration faced was as it preached to the world that we were pivoting and that we were re-balancing in Asia, if you did not have an economic component, which is what the TPP really stands for, the Asians would really not take you as quite seriously as they do now with the TPP and if it becomes a successful agreement.

So that we find the Obama administration really in some ways has come full circle, and this starts with the President himself who to his credit today, I think, is really, he said a year or so ago that he was all in for the United States as a Pacific power. He is, I think, all in for the TPP, and I congratulate him for that. Thank you.

[The prepared statement of Mr. Barfield follows:]

CONGRESSIONAL TESTIMONY

Statement before the
Subcommittee on Asia and the Pacific:
Committee on Foreign Affairs

"The Trans-Pacific Partnership and America's strategic role in Asia"

March 4, 2015

Claude Barfield, Ph.D.
Resident Scholar
American Enterprise Institute

The stakes for US trade policy have always reached beyond the economic realm...Trade is what most of international relations are about. For that reason trade policy is national security policy."
Thomas Schelling, Nobel Prize winner

Trade policy stands at the intersection of a nation's diplomatic and security strategies and its broad economic goals. Decisions regarding trade agreements, with both individual nations and groups of nations, are calculated to advance national strategic interests as well as the fortunes of domestic corporations and workers. Though not necessarily in conflict, security imperatives and economic realities exist in two very different universes, inhabited by very different constituencies and interest groups. With the exception of multilateral negotiations in the World Trade Organization – which deal exclusively with trade issues – bilateral, sub-regional, and regional trade negotiations inevitably are influenced and guided by collateral, compelling national priorities. Thus, in the case of the US, the Executive Office of the President, with input from diverse public agencies and private interest groups – for example, from the US State, Defense, Commerce, and Labor departments, as well as the US Environmental Protection Agency, and from outside groups and industries in manufacturing, services, agriculture, labor unions, and NGOs – calculate the economic and political tradeoffs inherent in the decisions to go forward with a particular bilateral or regional FTA. Though prime responsibility for the nitty-gritty of negotiations is in the hands of the US Trade Representative, these officials fulfill their responsibilities against a background of larger political, diplomatic, and security goals.

Political scientists also often refer to trade policy-making as a two-level game: that is, national leaders strive to forge an internal consensus on US trade negotiating goals and then must further attempt to achieve those goals at the international level. Inevitably, there are compromises in this process, forcing national leaders to return to the domestic level to defend the negotiating package. The recent history of US trade negotiations provides telling examples of the sometimes uneasy juxtaposition of diplomatic/security priorities and the two-level game in which domestic economic interests must be accommodated. For the United States, indeed, the difficult process of completing and ratifying FTAs with Colombia and Korea itself are cases in point. In both instances, there were strong diplomatic/security rationales to buttress an important ally in a dangerous region. Yet in both cases, US domestic conflicts delayed the advancement of US national interests for some years.

US Trade/Security Policy

From 1945 through the end of the 1980s, the US largely adhered to a two-track trade policy: multilateralism, embodied in membership in the GATT; and unilateralism/bilateralism, dictated by the substantive reality that the GATT disciplines did not include important trading sectors and issues. Thus, powerful domestic interests demanded that US policymakers pursue independent bilateral negotiations with key partners such as the European Community and Japan to achieve trade policy goals not covered by multilateral disciplines.

This truncated policy framework broadened greatly during the George H.W. Bush administration, when the end of the Cold War and the rise of regional economies around the EC and Japan produced a rethinking of the boundaries of US international economic policy. Then-Secretary of State James Baker emerged as the driving force behind a major reorientation of US trade and security policy. First, Baker stated that although the GATT would remain the top priority for US trade negotiations, "bilateral and minilateral systems may help move the world toward a more open system." NAFTA negotiations were the most immediate symbol of this US shift. In Asia, which is the primary focus of this article, Baker quickly responded favorably to a joint Australia-Japan proposal leading to the creation of the Asia-Pacific Economic Cooperation organization, or APEC. And he was immediately hostile to a proposal by then-Malaysian President Mahathir Mohamad for an East Asian Economic Caucus that would include only Asian nations and exclude the United States.

It was in response to Mahathir that Baker famously set forth what became an enduring US strategic position with regard to the region, when he vowed that the United States would oppose any "plan that drew a line down the middle of the Pacific," with the Unites States on one side of the line and Asian nations on the other. Baker stated later that while there were no immediate security challenges to US hegemony in Asia, his statement was intended as a declaration and projection of diplomatic and security power as well as a statement of national economic interest. Since Baker's original pronouncement, US economic and diplomatic/security goals in Asia have been inextricably linked.

The Clinton administration was fortunate to preside over the so-called "unipolar moment" in postwar history. The Cold War had ended; and in Asia, Japan had begun an extended period of stagnation, while China's subsequent economic and political power was still just over the horizon. In international relations, economic goals took priority, and the United States led in the upgrading of APEC and the establishment of the Bogor goals of free trade in the Asia-Pacific by 2010 for developed APEC nations, and by 2020 for developing APEC nations. It should be noted, however, that in concluding NAFTA and pursuing a Free Trade of the Americas agreement, the Clinton White House espoused strong political aims to buttress economic interests: to wit, supporting the emergence of viable democratic systems, first in Mexico but later throughout Latin America.

For the themes developed in this paper, the George W. Bush administration stands as a central focal point, in that more explicitly than prior administrations (and moreso than the Obama administration that succeeded it), Bush administration trade policy directly and publicly tied trade policy initiatives to broader US foreign policy and security goals. The administration also included Zoellick, who served as the US Trade Representative (USTR) during George W. Bush's first term and was a protégé of James Baker, who naturally viewed trade policy through the wider lens of US diplomatic goals. In speeches and congressional testimony, he candidly stated that in choosing FTA partners, the administration would seek "cooperation – or better – on foreign and security policy...Given that the US has international interests beyond trade, why not try to urge people to support our overall policies." Under President Bush, the US negotiated some 17 FTAs (bilateral and regional), in some cases largely for economic reasons (viz., Chile, Peru, and CAFTA); in other cases, clearly for political/diplomatic purposes (Bahrain, Oman, and Morocco, as well as others for a combination – viz., Singapore and Australia). Three FTAs (Korea, Colombia, Panama)—each of which represented a combined economic/security imperative—were negotiated by President Bush but went unratified by the US Congress at the end of his term.

The Obama Administration and the Asian "Pivot"

Though in many ways the foreign policy of the Obama administration has differed dramatically from that of the Bush administration, in both administrations diplomatic and security considerations played a large role in shaping trade policy. This was underscored by the decision of the Obama White House to assign major strategic and political trade decisions to the National Security Council, and not to the USTR. Further, the role of individual leadership in shaping US Asian policy forms a key element in the Obama administration, with Secretary Hillary Clinton's central focus on Asia providing a bookend to Secretary Baker's guiding vision two decade previously.

Asia: Trade and Economic Policy

As he entered office, President Obama seemed an unlikely candidate to push forward with a bold US trade agenda. Famously, in the campaign he had boasted that he opposed the NAFTA agreement and subsequent bilateral FTAs, and he led a Democratic party deeply divided by trade liberalization and globalization issues. Thus, for almost a year the US in effect had no trade policy. But by the end of 2009, a combination of economic imperatives and foreign policy challenges would impel a major turnaround on the trade front.

Though the financial crisis ebbed during 2009, the recession dragged on; and despite continuing Democratic congressional opposition, Obama turned to trade—and exports—to boost the flagging US economy. This resulted in a major National Export Initiative to boost US exports around the world, but particularly in the rapidly expanding Asian economies. Under the initiative, the president promised to double US exports over a five-year period.

Asia: The Pivot

Though economic factors were important, what more decisively shaped the course of Obama administration Asia policy was the rapidly shifting diplomatic and security conditions in the region. As former British Prime Minister Harold Macmillan is said to have replied when asked what could steer a government off its current course: "Events, dear boy, events." "Events" indeed explain the decisive "pivot" by the Obama administration in Asia, as well as the forward movement on the trade and economic front.

Within months after assuming office in 2009, North Korea heightened tension on the Korean peninsula and threatened South Korea, a US treaty ally, by first conducting an underground nuclear test, and then shooting off two rounds of short-range missile across the Sea of Japan. Pressure mounted immediately for a show of support for South Korea, resulting from the administration's own accounts in a decision by the president to announce a goal of completing negotiations on the stalled KORUS.

On a broader scale, even before the Obama administration took office, mainland China had hardened its attitude and diplomacy on a raft of disagreements and conflicts with its East Asia neighbors. Though not repudiating the mantra of a "peaceful rise," China's leaders became much more assertive in their relations with individual nations—as well as ultimately with ASEAN as an organization. In May 2009, just after the administration took office, Beijing published a map of the South China containing nine dashed lines in a U-shape that laid claim to over 80 percent of this maritime area. Subsequently, it clashed repeatedly with its neighbors inside this self-proclaimed perimeter—particularly the Philippines and Vietnam. In addition, the PRC grew bolder in contesting the claims of South Korea and Japan, respectively, in the Japan and East China seas.

The US Response

Secretary of State Clinton's first trip abroad was not—as had been traditional—to Europe, but to Asia. In speeches and testimony during the first months of the Obama administration, Clinton proclaimed with some bravado that the United States was "back" in Asia, vowing to pursue a "more rigorous commitment and engagement." To that end, she beefed up the economic resources and mission of the State Department and pressed for forward movement on US regional trade and investment issues. Within months, the US signed the Treaty of Amity and Commerce with ASEAN, paving the way for membership in the East Asian Summit. Since 2009, the secretary has made nine trips to Asia, more than to any other region of the world.

Obama's Trip to Asia

Statements and visits by secretaries of state and defense are important, but both the symbolic and substantive capstone of the US "pivot" came with President Obama's nine-day trip to Asia in November 2011. Starting in Hawaii as host to the APEC Leaders Meeting, the president went on to make major pronouncements and policy advances in Indonesia where he met with ASEAN leaders and became the first American president to join the East Asian Summit.

The president chose Australia to deliver his most important and far-reaching address reaffirming the US commitment to Asia—and to the Australian alliance. "The United States is a Pacific power, and we are here to stay," he averred, adding: "In the Asia Pacific in the 21st century, the United States of America is all in." Later in Darwin, the president and the prime minister announced a new security pact by which the US would deploy a rotating group of 2500 marines, establishing an important symbolic presence in maritime Southeast Asia.

From the outset of the trip in Hawaii, however, it was the TPP that created the "buzz" that would continue throughout remainder of the president's journey. With the (premature) announcement that a "framework" had been agreed to, the TPP moved to center stage as the most concrete symbol of renewed US leadership in the region. As noted above, this symbolism came with high risks. While a framework had been announced, TPP negotiations had yet to tackle the most difficult economic and political negotiating issues. But whatever the future outcome (see below), the president's imprimatur and his repeated reference to the negotiations as a cornerstone of US renewed leadership meant that the success or failure of these negotiations would be taken, for better or for worse, as a central symbol for the success or failure of US leadership and the long-term impact of the "pivot."

TPP

From the outset of the negotiations, however, the trans-Pacific pact has been hailed as the new model for a 21st Century trade agreement. The goal is to negotiate terms that go well beyond traditional FTAs and write rules for major inside-the-border barriers to competition. Thus in terms of the themes developed in this paper, the TPP has large geoeconomic implications: that is, if successful, it will provide the template and model for future FTAs around the world and, ultimately, for multinational negotiations in the WTO.

The most significant new (21st century) issues being debated include: new rules for state-owned- enterprises (SOEs); labor and environmental rules; intellectual property strictures; regulatory reform and coherence; government procurement liberalization; trade facilitation measures; supply chain management; and measures to promote trade by small- and medium-sized businesses. On regulatory reform, the overarching goal is the harmonization (or at least mutual recognition) of regulatory barriers that exert a major influence on international trade. Among the proposals discussed in the negotiating sessions are procedural rules for transparency; elimination of duplicative or overlapping regulations; restriction on anticompetitive practices; mutual recognition agreements for services and for health and safety measures. On SOEs, the goal is to promote "competitive neutrality" between commercial enterprises and government-owned entities, particularly in the areas of subsidization and regulatory discrimination.

Ironically, some of the most difficult substantive and political issues involve traditional "20th Century" points of contention such as existing tariffs and barriers on textiles and apparel, shoes, sugar, dairy products and cotton. For the big picture, the tradeoffs will consist of balancing 21 century demands by more advanced TPP members against the political needs of the less advanced TPP nations regarding these more traditional trading barriers.

The Strategic Overlay

Over and beyond the fascinating—and necessary–domestic interplay of the two-level game are larger geoeconomic and geostrategic forces, with wide-ranging implications for continued US leadership of both a more liberal trading system and regional order in the Asia Pacific.

RCEP: Geoeconomic Competition

Standing in the wings as competition for the TPP is the Regional Comprehensive Economic Partnership (RCEP), pushed by the PRC as an intra-Asian alternative. Launched in 2013—thought negotiations did not begin until well into 2013—RCEP is composed of the ASEAN Plus 6 nations: ASEAN, China, Japan, Korea, India, Australia and New Zealand. There is some overlap in membership with the TPP: Australia, New Zealand, Singapore, Malaysia, Brunei, and Vietnam are participating in both sets of negotiations.

In substance and in negotiating modes, TPP and RCEP stand in contrast to each other. First, unlike the TPP, where individual ASAEEAN nations negotiating separately, in RCEP ASEAN is represented as a single economic and political entity. Thus, RCEP from the outset will include the less developed ASEAN members (Laos, Cambodia, Myanmar) as well as somewhat more developed members such as Thailand, the Philippines, and Indonesia. In part, this membership difference—as well as the inclusion of ASEAN as a distinct entity—has dictated different negotiating ground rules. First, there will be a great deal of flexibility in the negotiating mode, which will be accomplished in a sequential manner or a single undertaking, or thought some other mixed modality. RCEP will also provide special and differential treatment to less-developed ASEAN member states. Finally, in contrast to the TPP, membership in RCEP is fixed and limited to the present 16 members (from outset TPP membership has been open-ended, allowing it to grow from five to the present twelve members).

Substantively, as compared to the deep integration goals of the TPP, the initial aims of RECP are much less ambitious. Three negotiating subgroups have been established in goods, services and investment; but it is not expected that the agreement will contain many of the "behind the scenes" non-tariff barrier liberalization that are the objects of the TPP negotiators. RCEP nations have pledged to reach agreement on major issues by the end of 2015, though most observers hold that this goal is unrealistic. However, even if real substantive advances only come in later years, RCEP stands as a serious, intra-Asian regional alternative to the TPP should those negotiation falter or fail.

Strategic Challenges

Over the past several years, even as TPP negotiations have deepened and moved toward an endpoint (whether successful or not), the strategic and security situation in East Asia has become ever more fraught. Further, as new challenges have arisen, there have been growing concerns among allies and trading partners regarding US steadfastness and staying power in the region. These fears have stemmed from disparate sources. Despite the vow to "rebalance" US security forces toward the Asia Pacific, with 60 percent of US naval assets in the Pacific by 2020, Asian leaders are fully cognizant that this is 60 percent of a declining US defense budget. They are also aware of the political stalemate that has often produced a paralysis in domestic policymaking.

Beyond this reality, over the past year—and certainly over the past few weeks and months, distractions and crisis in other regions of the world—the Ukraine and Russia, and at this writing direct military actions to counter ISIS in Iraq and Syria—have driven home the fact that US worldwide obligations can overwhelm its strategic regional goals in East Asia.

Meanwhile, in East Asia itself recent, China's challenges to the existing order have risen sharply. Seemingly unconcerned about its political image and the contradictions to its often proclaimed "peaceful rise," Beijing has picked or exacerbated quarrels with a number of its East Asian neighbors. Many of these controversies, with accompanying Chinese bullying tactics, have centered on disputed maritime borders and jurisdiction, including jousting with Japan over the Senkakyu Islands in the East China Sea; with Vietnam over the Paracel Islands in the South China Sea; with the Philippines, Vietnam, and Malaysia over the Spratly Islands; and with the Philippines over the Scarborough Shoal. In recent months, China has upped the ante by sending a semi-permanent oil rig into waters around the Paracel Islands. Throughout the period, Beijing has adamantly refused to call a halt to development of the disputed maritime territories or to seriously enter into negotiations for a code of conduct or some form of joint development of the disputed areas.

Finally, with the unilateral declaration of an Air Defense Identification Zone in the East China Sea, the PRC has directly thrown down the gauntlet not only to its neighbors in Asia but also to the United States and its long-standing defense of the doctrine of the freedom of the seas. The US has refused to recognize the Chinese ADZ and declined to notify Beijing of flights across the disputed area.

The point of this brief diplomatic and security rundown is to underscore that, with the TPP as a central and most concrete symbol of the US "pivot" to Asia, the repercussions of a failure to carry the trade agreement to a successful juncture will ripple out well beyond economic consequences.

Singapore and its leaders, going back to Lee Kuan Yew, have always exhibited the most savvy and sophisticated understanding of the US leadership role and the symbolic and concrete importance of the TPP in the East Asian firmament and order. This tradition was carried on several weeks ago, when Singapore Prime Minister Lee Hsien Loong, warned of the consequences of TPP failure. He stated: "We have promised to conclude...three years in a row, I think this is our last chance to fulfill our promise...(or) face further delays of an indefinite nature." He further stressed that the US Asian pivot must have an economic as well as military component: "If you don't finish TPP you just giving the game away (to China)...If you don't promote trade what are you promoting? What does it mean when you say you are a Pacific power? That just does not make sense."

President Obama understands this; for as he stated in the State of the Union address to Congress: "China wants to write the rules for the world's fastest growing region. That would put our workers and businesses at a disadvantage. Why would we let that happen? We should write those rules. That's why I am asking both parties to give me trade promotion authority to protect American workers with strong trade deals from Asia to Europe that aren't just free, but also are fair."

 American Enterprise Institute

Trade Promotion Authority: A winning bargain for Congress and the president

Claude Barfield
February 19, 2015 4:16 pm | *The American*

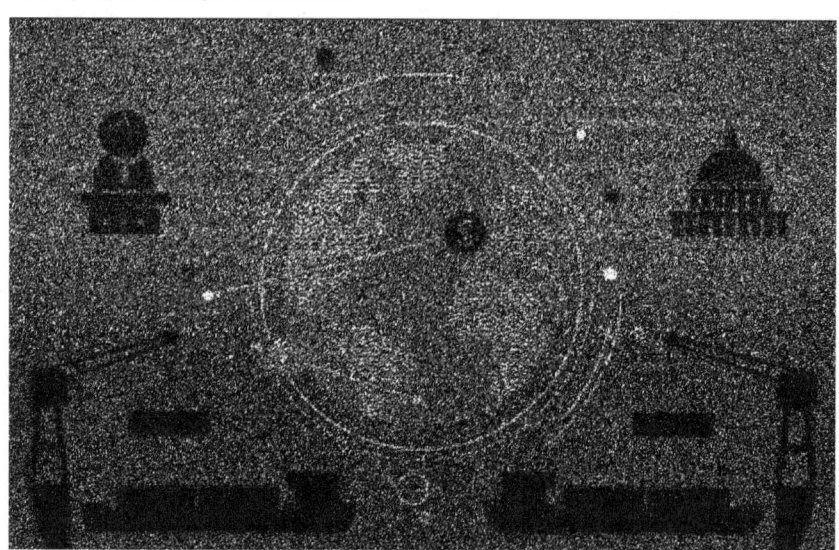

As Congress takes on new legislation to speed up trade agreements, the debate will seek to find a balance between the authority of Congress over trade policy and the necessity that the president craft agreements that further US economic interests. This commentary will attempt to sort fact from fiction and to provide a deeper historical context for the current struggle.

Trade Promotion Authority (or Fast Track Authority, under an earlier name) establishes a co-equal partnership between the president and Congress to expedite passage of legislation implementing trade agreements. The essential bargain goes as follows: the president agrees to negotiate trade agreements pursuant to objectives and priorities established by the Congress; in return, Congress agrees to an expedited up-or-down vote on the agreement and implementing legislation, without amendment. First established by Congress in 1974, the joint procedure has been renewed some six times under both Republican and Democratic presidents, and by Congresses controlled by both Republicans and Democrats, or divided between the parties. While the specific congressionally mandated objectives and priorities have evolved over time, the basic procedural framework and bargain have remained in place.

A brief history of TPA. Unlike many other governments in which the executive exercises strong or complete control over international economic relations, in the United States it is Congress that is granted full and final authority over trade policy. Article I Section 8 states simply and decisively that Congress shall have the power: "To regulate Commerce with foreign nations." For 150 years, Congress exercised control of US trade policy through passage of tariff legislation, that is, taxes on foreign goods at the border. In 1934, however, Congress — wanting to rid itself of the endless petty demands on individual tariffs — granted the president authority to reduce tariffs on a reciprocal basis with other nations within pre-approved levels.

All of this worked well during the first rounds of multilateral trade negotiations under the General Agreement on Trade and Tariffs in the 1940s and 1950s. During the Kennedy Round in the 1960s, however, trade negotiators moved beyond tariffs to tackle nontariff barriers to trade such as antidumping and regulatory regimes. This would ultimately force changes in domestic laws, and, at first, Congress balked and refused to act on these US commitments. At that point, US trading partners in turn demanded that the United States establish a system that produced an up-or-down vote on the final terms of future trade agreements (including implementing legislation) negotiated by the president and his team.

Fast Track Authority. In the Trade Act of 1974, Congress established so-called Fast Track (Trade Promotion) Authority. As noted above, the TPA authority has been repeatedly renewed since 1974, and the basic procedural framework has remained largely the same. Over the next few weeks, the Republican congressional leadership has promised to produce the latest version of TPA, hopefully with some support from Democrats. Republican leaders have stated that the new authorization will follow closely the details of last year's Bipartisan Trade Promotion Act of 2014.

The 2014 BTPA reflected increased congressional demands for greater participation in the FTA negotiating process, without impinging on the president's broad executive power over foreign economic policy. With regard to consultation and notification, the act provided for:

- 90-day congressional notification before entering into negotiations for a new FTA.
- 90-day congressional notification before concluding negotiations for an FTA.
- Establishment of Congressional Advisory Groups in both houses that would preside over timely briefing during the course of the negotiations and be given access to all relevant documents. Membership would include select members of the Ways and Means and Finance Committees, as well as the chairmen of committees with jurisdiction over laws affected by the FTA.
- Creation of a broader Designated Congressional Advisors group, consisting of members who have petitioned for such a designation and received permission from relevant committee chairmen.
- A mandate to the Ways and Means and Finance Committee to establish a detailed system and timetable for consultation with the US trade representative (USTR).
- Enhanced transparency for the public by directing the USTR to develop specific plans for public outreach and consultation. (It should be noted that the USTR already has conducted some 1,600 briefings and meetings with NGOs, individual companies, and trade associations, and congressional staff.)
- The USTR, upon request of any member of Congress, must provide all pertinent documents in a timely fashion, including when available the final terms of a proposed FTA.

Further, in a January 30 speech at the American Enterprise Institute, Senate Finance Committee Chairman, Orrin Hatch (R-Utah) outlined several additional safeguards that will be included in the 2015 TPA process: implementing bills would include only provisions that are "strictly necessary and proper," with "strictly" tightening the scope of such legislation; secret side deals would be outlawed in future trade agreements; and any changes to the agreement made after TPA had expired but before Congress has voted on the agreement would be placed outside the TPA process. He also promised that Congress would continue to insist on transparency throughout the process: there would be no "surprises" to the Congress or the public.

Expedited procedures. As noted above, the administration must give 90 days' notice to the Congress before concluding an agreement. At that point, the USTR and the Ways and Means and Finance Committees (along with other committee of jurisdiction) begin joint work on crafting implementing legislation, including any changes to US law required by the agreement. The two committees hold so-called "mock markups" of the implementing legislation to work out any differences with the administration; and, should it be necessary, they hold "mock conferences" to iron out any differences between the two houses. There is no statutory time limit on this segment of the process.

With final implementing legislation agreed, the clock starts ticking again when the president formally submits a bill. The two committees have 45 session days to discharge the bill to the floor and the full Congress. Once it reaches the floor of each house, debate is limited to 20 hours, with no amendments allowed.

Mandated negotiating objectives and priorities. Beyond the ultimate ability to reject proposed FTAs, Congress's most potent power to dictate the substance of future agreements comes through the negotiating mandates it gives to the president when it passes the TPA. At this point in time — with more than a decade having passed since Congress last weighed in — careful attention will be paid to new negotiating objectives that reflect the vastly changed economic and technological landscape that has emerged since passage of the 2002 TPA. The usual format of the TPA is to divide it into categories of general objectives, more specific objectives, and finally other priorities. Some objectives have been included since the advent of the TPA: these include details regarding market access for goods, services, and agricultural products. Within these general categories, Congress often adds specific market access demands: viz., food safety and animal and plant health laws and regulation. Issues related to investment (and investment adjudication) and intellectual property will be updated to reflect current concerns. The TPA will also add a significant number of new issues, including rules for state-owned enterprises, regulatory reform and coherence, rules for an open Internet and freedom of data flows, restrictions on localization, and IP rules for new biologic drugs. The mandates concerning new issues are of paramount importance, as in these areas Congress has previously given no indication of its priorities.

> Careful attention will be paid to new negotiating objectives that reflect the vastly changed economic and technological landscape that has emerged since passage of the 2002 TPA.

There is a close and direct link between the objectives Congress mandates in the TPA and the consultation/reporting sections of the bill. In the pending Trans-Pacific Partnership negotiations, the legislators have carefully monitored the progression of the negotiating sessions; and they fully expect that the administration will attempt to bring to fruition the major goals set forth in the TPA — though there is also the (unspoken) knowledge that a final FTA package will contain areas where the United States has had to compromise in order to get a result that all 12 nations can agree to.

Partisan conflicts and the TPA. Since the mid-1990s, partisan conflicts over trade policy have spilled over into the TPA legislative process. It should be noted, however, that these conflicts are not centered on the TPA procedural executive-legislative compromise, but rather on disagreements over what issues and substantive mandates should be included in the TPA and subsequently in future FTAs. The most difficult issues coming forward from the 1990s have concerned the extent to which FTAs will include mandates in the areas of labor rights and environmental protection. Other contentious areas include IP for pharmaceuticals, investor-state dispute settlement, health and safety measures, and currency manipulation. In the current process, the administration is working to find some accommodation that will (minimally) satisfy various interest groups and constituencies.

For labor and environment, however, a 2007 compromise between the Bush administration and the Democratic Congress will dictate the language. In the so-called May 10th agreement, it was decided that both labor and environmental issues would be included in future agreements and subject to the regular dispute settlement provisions. Further, with regard to labor rights, nations will be expected to live up to the 1998 ILO Declaration on Fundamental Principles of Rights at Work. Unlike actual ILO Conventions on labor rights, the Declaration is not legally enforceable, but merely a hortatory document. Republicans had adamantly opposed obligations related to the ILO Conventions, as those would have forced wholesale revision of US labor laws.

On the environment, the May 10th agreement stipulates that FTA signatories must sign up to a group of UN environmental treaties, including those dealing with ozone depletion, endangered species, marine pollution, wetlands, tropical tuna, and Antarctic marine resources.

Constitutional questions and the executive balance of power. Controversies over the basic constitutionality of the TPA process, as well as the balance of power between the executive and the legislative branches of government, have been raised from the outset, and are looming again in the current struggle over passage of new TPA legislation. Both representatives from the Democratic left and the Tea Party Republican right have publicly expressed reservations about the legislation and the process. Opposition from the Democratic left wing is actually a cover for larger opposition to trade deals, particularly from labor and environmental interest groups. For conservative Republicans, however, there are real — if rebuttable — constitutional concerns. These Republicans have also been in the forefront of challenging what they consider the overreach of the executive branch under President Obama.

> The TPA will add a significant number of new issues, including rules for state-owned enterprises, regulatory reform and coherence, rules for an open Internet and freedom of data flows, restrictions on localization, and IP rules for new biologic drugs.

When the 2002 TPA was being considered, the same questions were raised by some Republicans. At that time, two legal scholars with impeccable conservative credentials, former Attorney General Edwin Meese and Judge Robert Bork, gave opinions supporting TPA constitutionality and the pragmatic balance between the executive and the legislature.

Meese wrote:

> [The TPA legislation] is clearly constitutional because Congress retains the right to approve or reject all future trade agreements. It might be unconstitutional if Congress tried to delegate its authority to approve the final deal — but that is not at issue ... The Constitution grants to each house of Congress the authority to establish its own rules of procedure, and it makes perfect sense for Congress to limit itself to straight up-or-down votes on certain resolutions, such as base closures and its own adjournment motions.

US sovereignty. Meese also dealt with questions raised regarding US sovereignty and ruling by international bodies. He noted:

> Future trade deals would not be unconstitutional, nor would they undermine US sovereignty, if they contained an agreement to submit some disputes to an international tribunal for initial determination. The United States will always have the ultimate say over what its domestic laws provide .... A ruling by an international tribunal that calls a U.S. law into question could have no domestic effect unless Congress changes the law to comply with the ruling.

In that regard, every TPA has included clauses that reinforce this sovereignty principle, such as:

> No provision of any trade agreement entered into under the TPA that is inconsistent with any law of the United States, or any State, or any locality of the United States, shall have any effect.

> Nor shall any provision of a TPA prevent the United States, or any State, or any locality from amending its laws.

Final Thoughts

The congressional fingerprint is on every step in the TPA process, from the framing of mandated trade objectives and priorities, to continuous consultation and feedback, to the crafting of implementing legislation, and finally, to the up-or-down final decision on an FTA.

US sovereignty is closely guarded and reinforced through specific clauses that nullify any section of an agreement that is inconsistent with US law. Further, a congressional vote on TPA is *not* a vote in favor of FTAs pursuant to its mandates. Congress can and will exercise an independent judgment as to whether these agreements reflect its mandates to the president and are in the interest of the American people.

Without TPA, the United States would not be able to achieve its own negotiating goals, as our trading partners would hold back their own bottom-line compromises out of fear that the president and the USTR could not guarantee the steadfastness and good faith of the US political process.

Claude Barfield is a resident scholar at the American Enterprise Institute.

This article was found online at:
http://www.aei.org/publication/trade-promotion-authority-winning-bargain-congress-president/

Mr. SALMON. Thank you.
Ms. Overby?

STATEMENT OF MS. TAMI OVERBY, SENIOR VICE PRESIDENT FOR ASIA, U.S. CHAMBER OF COMMERCE

Ms. OVERBY. Thank you very much for the opportunity to speak on behalf of the U.S. Chamber of Commerce and share our views of our members. I believe all of us can agree that economic growth and creating good jobs are the nation's top economic priorities.

Approximately 17 million Americans are unemployed, under-employed or have given up looking for work. Participation in the workforce stands at 63 percent, the lowest level since 1978, reflecting a significant level of discouragement. There are many policy options Congress will consider to improve this dire situation. International trade should be prominent among them. After all, outside our borders are markets that represent 80 percent of the world's purchasing power, 92 percent of its economic power, and 95 percent of its consumers.

The most immediate and important trade opportunity before us is the topic of this hearing, the 12-country Trans-Pacific Partnership Agreement. This agreement would link countries in North and Latin America with important markets in Asia representing nearly 40 percent of global GDP. As U.S. companies scour the globe looking for consumers, Asia stands out as brimming with opportunity. Over the last two decades, the region's middle class grew by 2 billion people and their spending power is greater than ever. That number is expected to rise by another 1.2 billion people by 2020.

According to the IMF, the world economy will grow by over $21 trillion in the next 5 years with nearly half of that growth in Asia. U.S. businesses, workers and farmers need better access to those lucrative markets if they are going to share in this dramatic growth.

But American companies are falling rapidly behind in Asia. While U.S. exports to Asia increased steadily from 2000 to 2010, America's share of the region's imports declined by about 43 percent. In fact, the growth in U.S. exports to Asia lagged overall U.S. growth in that period.

One reason many companies have lost market share in Asia is that many countries maintain steep barriers against U.S. exports. A typical Southeast Asian country imposes tariffs that are five times higher than the U.S. average while its duties on our ag products soar into the triple digits. In addition, a web of non-tariff and regulatory barriers block market access in many of these countries. Trade agreements are crafted to overcome these barriers, and without them U.S. goods and services and the workers that provide them will continue to be blocked from these lucrative opportunities.

But the U.S. disadvantages do not end there. Other countries are plowing ahead with trade deals that are leaving America on the outside looking in. China, India and 14 countries are negotiating a trade deal called the Regional Comprehensive Economic Partnership that does not include America. This agreement does threaten to draw a line down the Pacific and put American workers, farmers and businesses that you represent on the wrong side of history.

The TPP is not only America's best chance, it is our only chance to ensure that America is not left out as these countries in the most economically dynamic region of the world pursue new trade accords among themselves. Unlike RCEP or the many 350-plus trade agreements already in force around the globe, the TPP promises to set high new standards and establish new rules for trade and investment that will generate greater benefits for all participating countries.

TPP is a chance to introduce ground breaking disciplines in emerging areas so that trade and investment rules can keep pace with a rapidly evolving global economy and increasingly sophisticated behind-the-border measures that governments are increasingly using to block our access and obstruct market-based competition.

In order to provide American workers, farmers and companies with these opportunities, Congress must first approve legislation to renew trade promotion authority. With TPA we simply cannot enter into new agreements. We are excited to see that Congress and the administration are focused on TPA and working hard to prepare legislation to renew it in the coming weeks. TPA is a critical element of an economic policy which spurs economic growth and job creation in America.

The agenda is clear. The U.S. cannot afford to sit on the sidelines while others design a new trade architecture for Asia. A comprehensive, ambitious and enforceable market opening TPP has the potential to create an explosion of trade and new American jobs and would demonstrate continued U.S. leadership across this important region. It is an exciting vision which on the right terms can be an economic shot in the arm for the United States and for our friends and allies in the region. It can send a clear, unmistakable message that Americans' leadership is in the Pacific to stay.

The U.S. Chamber of Commerce looks forward to working with the members of this committee to secure a commercially strong TPP as soon as possible. Thank you.

[The prepared statement of Ms. Overby follows:]

Statement of the U.S. Chamber of Commerce

**ON: The Trans-Pacific Partnership:
Prospects for Greater U.S. Trade**

**TO: U.S. House of Representatives Committee
on Foreign Affairs
Subcommittee on Asia and the Pacific**

**BY: Tami Overby, Senior Vice President for Asia
U.S. Chamber of Commerce**

DATE: March 4, 2015

1615 H Street NW | Washington, DC | 20062

The Chamber's mission is to advance human progress through an economic,
political and social system based on individual freedom,
incentive, initiative, opportunity and responsibility.

24

The U.S. Chamber of Commerce is the world's largest business federation representing the interests of more than three million businesses of all sizes, sectors, and regions, as well as state and local chambers and industry associations.

More than 96% of Chamber member companies have fewer than 100 employees, and many of the nation's largest companies are also active members. We are therefore cognizant not only of the challenges facing smaller businesses, but also those facing the business community at large.

Besides representing a cross-section of the American business community with respect to the number of employees, major classifications of American business—e.g., manufacturing, retailing, services, construction, wholesalers, and finance—are represented. The Chamber has membership in all 50 states.

The Chamber's international reach is substantial as well. We believe that global interdependence provides opportunities, not threats. In addition to the American Chambers of Commerce abroad, an increasing number of our members engage in the export and import of both goods and services and have ongoing investment activities. The Chamber favors strengthened international competitiveness and opposes artificial U.S. and foreign barriers to international business.

Positions on issues are developed by Chamber members serving on committees, subcommittees, councils, and task forces. Nearly 1,900 businesspeople participate in this process.

On the occasion of this hearing of the House Foreign Affairs Subcommittee on Asia and the Pacific on "The Trans-Pacific Partnership (TPP): Prospects for Greater U.S. Trade," the U.S. Chamber of Commerce is pleased to take this opportunity to offer its own views and those of its members in support of the TPP and renewal of Trade Promotion Authority (TPA). The Chamber is the world's largest business federation, representing the interests of more than three million businesses of all sizes, sectors, and regions, as well as state and local chambers and industry associations.

In the Chamber's view, reinvigorating economic growth and creating good jobs are the nation's top priorities. More than 17 million Americans are unemployed, underemployed, or have given up looking for work. Participation in the workforce stands near 62%, the lowest since 1978, reflecting a significant level of discouragement.

World trade must play a central role in reaching this job-creation goal. After all, outside our borders are markets that represent 80% of the world's purchasing power, 92% of its economic growth, and 95% of its consumers. The resulting opportunities are immense, and many Americans are already seizing them. One in three manufacturing jobs depends on exports, and one in three acres on American farms is planted for hungry consumers overseas.

Nor is trade important only to big companies. Often overlooked in the U.S. trade debate is the fact that 98% of the 300,000 U.S. companies that export their products are small and medium-sized enterprises (SMEs), and they account for one-third of U.S. merchandise exports, according to the U.S. Department of Commerce. In fact, the number of SMEs that export has more than doubled over the past 15 years.

The bottom line is simple: If America fails to look abroad, our workers and businesses will miss out on huge opportunities. Our standard of living and our standing in the world will suffer. With so many Americans out of work, opening markets abroad to the products of American workers, farmers, and companies is a higher priority than ever before.

The Problem: Foreign Tariffs and Other Trade Barriers

The chief obstacle to achieving greater economic benefits from trade is the complex array of foreign barriers to American exports. While the United States receives substantial benefits from trade, there is more than a grain of truth in the observation that the international playing field is unfairly tilted against American workers. The U.S. market is largely open to imports from around the world, but other countries continue to levy tariffs on U.S. exports that in some cases are quite high. Further, foreign governments have erected other kinds of barriers against U.S. goods and services that both block access and distort competition.

Americans rightly sense that this status quo is unfair to U.S. workers, farmers and businesses. U.S. exporters face higher tariffs abroad than nearly all our trade competitors. The United States received a rank of 130th among 138 economies in terms of "tariffs faced" by its exports, according to the World Economic Forum's Global Enabling Trade Report. That means U.S. exporters are often at a marked disadvantage to our competitors based in other countries.

No one wants to go into a basketball game down by a dozen points from the tip-off—but that is exactly what American exporters do every day. These barriers are particularly burdensome for America's small- and medium-sized exporters. The U.S. Chamber believes that American workers, farmers and businesses must be allowed to operate on a level playing field when it comes to trade.

Benefits of U.S. Trade Agreements

The good news is that America's trade agreements do a great job creating a level playing field—and tremendous commercial gains are the proof in the pudding. According to data from the U.S. Department of Commerce, nearly half of U.S. exports go to countries with which the United States has free-trade agreements (FTAs) even though they represent just 6% of the world's population. By tearing down foreign barriers to U.S. products, these agreements have a proven ability to make big markets even out of small economies.

To settle once and for all the debate over whether these FTAs have benefitted American workers and companies, the U.S. Chamber recently released a study entitled *Opening Markets, Creating Jobs: Estimated U.S. Employment Effects of Trade with FTA Partners*. The study examined U.S. FTAs implemented with a total of 14 countries. It employed a widely used economic model known as the Global Trade Analysis Project (GTAP), which is also used by the numerous federal agencies, the U.S. International Trade Commission, and the World Trade Organization (WTO).

The results of this comprehensive study are impressive: 17.7 million American jobs depend on trade with these 14 countries; of this total, 5.4 million U.S. jobs are supported by the increase in trade generated by the FTAs. No other budget neutral initiative undertaken by the U.S. government has generated jobs on a scale comparable to these FTAs, with the exception of the multilateral trade liberalization begun in 1947.

The trade balance is a poor measure of the success of these agreements, but the trade deficit is often cited by trade skeptics as a principal reason why the United States should not negotiate additional FTAs. However, taken as a group, the United States ran a trade surplus with its FTA partner countries in 2012 and 2013, and while services trade data for 2014 is not yet available, this surplus has plainly continued. In fact, the United States has recorded a trade surplus in manufactured goods with its FTA partner countries for each of the past seven years, according to the U.S. Department of Commerce. This surplus reached $27 billion in 2009 and had expanded to $61 billion by 2013.

Broadly, trade has been a lifeline for the U.S. economy in recent years. Exports have risen by more than 50% over the past five years, and one-third of the American jobs created in this period are in industries that depend on trade. However, the picture is not all rosy. U.S. trade is up, but we are still falling behind our competition. The U.S. share of global exports fell from 18% in 2000 to 12% in 2010. What can we do about this?

The Solution: The Trans-Pacific Partnership

The most immediate trade opportunity before us, and the topic of this hearing, is the 12-country Trans-Pacific Partnership (TPP) agreement. Launched over five years ago, these negotiations include Australia, Brunei, Canada, Chile, Japan, Malaysia, Mexico, New Zealand, Peru, Singapore, Vietnam and the United States and represent nearly 40% of global GDP.

As U.S. companies scour the globe for consumers, the booming Asia-Pacific region stands out. Over the last two decades, the region's middle class grew by 2 billion people, and their spending power is greater than ever. That number is expected to rise by another 1.2 billion by 2020. According to the International Monetary Fund, the world economy will grow by $21.6 trillion over the next five years, and nearly half of that growth will be in Asia.

U.S. businesses and workers need better access to those lucrative markets if they are going to share in this dramatic growth. But U.S. companies are rapidly falling behind in the Asia-Pacific. While U.S. exports to the Asia-Pacific market steadily increased from 2000 to 2010, America's share of the region's imports declined by about 43%, according to the think tank Third Way. In fact, excluding China, East Asia in 2014 purchased a smaller share of U.S. exports in 2014 than it did five years earlier, despite a 54% increase in total U.S. merchandise exports in that period.

One reason U.S. companies have lost market share in the Asia-Pacific region is that many countries maintain steep barriers against U.S. exports. A typical Southeast Asian country imposes tariffs that are five times higher than the U.S. average while its duties on agricultural products soar into the triple digits. In addition, a web of nontariff and regulatory barriers block market access in many countries. Trade agreements are crafted to overcome these barriers, and without them, U.S. goods and services—and the U.S. workers that provide them—will continue to be blocked from these lucrative opportunities.

However, the U.S. disadvantage does not end there. Other countries are plowing ahead with trade deals that are leaving the United States on the outside, looking in. For example, China, India and 14 other countries are negotiating a trade deal called the Regional Comprehensive Economic Partnership (RCEP) that does not include the United States. Broadly, the number of trade accords between Asian countries surged from three in 2000 to more than 50 in 2011, with some 80 more in the pipeline. Meanwhile, the United States has just three trade agreements in Asia.

The Trans-Pacific Partnership (TPP) is America's best and only chance to ensure the United States is not stuck on the outside—looking in—as the countries in the most economically dynamic region of the world pursue new trade accords among themselves.

Working closely with the Office of the U.S. Trade Representative (USTR), the Chamber has led the business community's advocacy for an ambitious, high-standard, commercially meaningful TPP agreement that eliminates or substantially reduces tariffs on agricultural and industrial goods. By engaging in a free trade agreement, we will not only knock down those barriers and open the door for American companies, but we will set a model for liberalization that has the potential to be adopted across the region.

High Standards, New Disciplines

According to the World Trade Organization (WTO), 398 bilateral or plurilateral FTAs are in force around the globe today. Unlike most of these other agreements, the TPP promises to set a new standard for trade and investment that will generate greater benefits for all participating countries. It is a chance to introduce ground-breaking disciplines in new areas so that trade and investment norms can keep pace with the rapidly evolving global economy and the behind-the-border measures that governments are increasingly using to block access and obstruct market-based competition.

In a statement issued in Honolulu in November 2011, the leaders of the TPP countries committed that this agreement will be:

> "... *a model for ambition for other free trade agreements in the future, forging close linkages among our economies, enhancing our competitiveness, benefitting our consumers and supporting the creation and retention of jobs, higher living standards, and the reduction of poverty in our countries.*"

Only by embracing open and competitive markets will we be able to truly level the playing field and realize the potential of the TPP agreement. Indeed, whenever one party in a trade negotiation excludes a given commodity or sector from an agreement, others invariably follow suit, limiting its reach. All TPP members—including the United States—must commit to open access across agriculture, manufacturing, and services, without exclusions. Carving out specific commodities, products, or sectors risks setting a negative precedent which will ultimately expose U.S. companies to similar treatment by our trading partners.

In addition to being comprehensive in scope, the rules of the TPP must be crafted in a way which protects U.S. exports and investors and promotes new growth in emerging sectors and markets.

Investment

U.S. firms that invest overseas are more globally competitive, export more, invest more in research and development in the United States, and pay their workers more compared to firms that serve only domestic markets. Additionally, multinationals' investments abroad serve as the gateway to the global economy for American small and medium-size businesses as they purchase 90% of their intermediate inputs from other U.S. companies.

The TPP must include gold standard obligations that support an open investment climate. These obligations should ensure companies have the freedom to own and control their investments, assurances that foreign direct investment receives fair and non-discriminatory treatment, and an expectation that host governments will adhere to rule of law. TPP parties must agree to uphold contract and property rights, prohibit discrimination against foreign companies, avoid onerous performance requirements as conditions for investment, and provide recourse to investor-State arbitration as a mechanism for settling dispute. Any derogation from these principles will be inconsistent with the ambition of the TPP leaders and unacceptable to U.S. industry.

Intellectual Property

One U.S. priority is to ensure the TPP protects intellectual property (IP), which plays a vital role in driving economic growth, jobs, and competitiveness. According to the U.S. Department of Commerce, IP-intensive companies account for more than $5 trillion of U.S. GDP, drive 60% of U.S. exports, and support 40 million American jobs.

For the United States to remain the most innovative economy on Earth, we must ensure that our IP-intensive industries remain confident that copyrights, patents, and trademarks will be enforced. Policies that protect and enforce IP rights abroad are essential to advancing America's competitiveness and export growth and creating high-quality, high-paying American jobs. In the TPP, U.S. negotiators must continue to press for robust IP protection and enforcement provisions that build on the U.S-Korea Free Trade Agreement and provide 12 years of data protection for biologic medicines consistent with U.S. law.

Additionally, the TPP must provide enhanced protections for trade secrets, which are critical to the competitiveness and strength of many U.S. companies across sectors as diverse as manufacturing, climate change technologies, chemicals, defense, biotech, IT services, and food and beverages. The TPP must prevent governments from masquerading industrial policy as competition policy through forced licensing of trade secrets solely because a trade secret owner refused to grant an unconditional license to a third party that wants or needs access to proprietary information to innovate and/or compete. This bright line between the right to keep proprietary information secret and competition enforcement should be articulated as a matter of Administration policy, advocated overseas on a regular basis, and included in the TPP.

State-Owned Enterprises

U.S investors and exporters are increasingly disadvantaged by the unfair practices of companies that are owned and assisted by governments. State-owned enterprises (SOEs) engaged in commercial transactions are increasingly distorting competition and allowing governments to circumvent their multilateral and bilateral trade and investment obligations. The TPP represents a precedent-setting opportunity to establish a basic set of rules for fair play that would place state-owned commercial companies on an equal footing with private sector competitors and ensure that commercial actors have the same opportunities for market access. We understand that government involvement in the marketplace will always be present in various forms and to various degrees within each country, but in order to prevent an undermining of trade commitments, anti-competitive SOE behavior and government favoritism toward commercial SOEs must be held in check.

Regulatory Coherence

As tariff rates have been lowered around the world, exporters and importers are left to deal with the emerging barriers of behind-the-border regulations which can impede trade and investment flows. Regulatory inconsistencies, conflicting standards and duplicative testing requirements can diminish the benefits of trade agreements, resulting in fewer jobs and less growth and competition. These inconsistent regimes across countries at times represent a pernicious form of both unintentional and intentional protectionism.

At the suggestion of the Chamber's Center for Global Regulatory Cooperation, the TPP partner countries have agreed to address regulatory barriers through a new horizontal chapter. The TPP's chapter on regulatory coherence presents an opportunity to align regulatory best practices among signatories to the agreement with the aim of minimizing unnecessary regulatory divergence. Doing so will help avoid the creation of new non-tariff barriers by calling for increased regulatory cooperation between U.S. regulators and their foreign counterparts across the TPP countries.

The TPP will encourage our trading partners to follow the principles that underlie U.S. administrative law and which are hallmarks of the APEC-OECD joint regulatory checklist. These principles include increased transparency and public participation, evidence-based regulation, accountability under the law, and impartiality. These basic disciplines will help to ensure that TPP regulators do not use regulations and standards as tools to unfairly restrict or hinder the competitiveness of U.S. companies.

Supply Chain

Trade facilitation is critically important to the trade community and the economic competitiveness of businesses. Manufacturers, retailers, and other businesses rely on the efficiency of the supply chain for their products and services in a just-in-time delivery environment. In order to ensure that the market openings are reached, we need to promote trade facilitation and get away from the errors of the past.

Chokepoints—such as excessive customs mandates, ineffective security mandates, and inadequate infrastructure—can have the same detrimental impact on the flow of trade. These hidden costs contribute to trade inefficiencies and can impose costs as high as 15% of the product value (OECD). In many countries, the benefits of improving trade facilitation could be as high as eliminating tariffs. A seamless TPP supply chain would unleash growth for a wide variety of businesses, especially small and medium-size companies, by connecting them to international markets. Trade facilitation enables economic growth, creates jobs, decreases the transaction costs of trade, and is critical to reaching the full potential of a TPP.

Cross Border Data Flows

The movement of electronic information across borders, including via cloud computing, is critical to the success of businesses operating in the today's global market. U.S. companies are increasingly using digital platforms to reach and sell to new customers in the TPP countries and around the world. Business, financial, insurance, information, communication, education, entertainment, retail and other services rely heavily on digital data and information flows, and many of these services act as enablers for the rest of the economy.

To accommodate this growing area of trade, the TPP agreement must ensure that enterprises and individuals can move and maintain information and data across borders in a reliable and secure manner. It is therefore critical that the TPP negotiations ensure that trade and investment rules promote, rather than inhibit, the growth of the digital economy. A successful TPP agreement must promote rules that are consistent with international best practices, are transparent, and allow businesses the flexibility to transact business through e-commerce platforms without establishing a commercial presence in each country.

* * *

In short, completing the TPP would pay huge dividends for the United States. The agreement would significantly improve U.S. companies' access to the Asia-Pacific region, which is projected to import nearly $10 trillion worth of goods in 2020. A study by the Peterson Institute for International Economics estimates the trade agreement could boost U.S. exports by $124 billion by 2025, and it could support hundreds of thousands of American jobs.

Trade Promotion Authority

First, however, Congress must approve legislation to renew Trade Promotion Authority (TPA). TPA is a vital tool to help Americans sell their goods and services to the 95% of the world's customers living outside our borders. Without TPA, we simply cannot enter into new trade agreements. We are pleased to see that Congress is preparing to consider legislation to renew TPA, which promises to spur economic growth and job creation at home.

The case for TPA is simple. In today's tough international markets, we need our trade negotiators to tear down the foreign tariffs and other barriers that too often shut out U.S products. However, to secure new growth-creating trade pacts such as the TPP, Congress must first approve TPA.

While the Constitution gives the president authority to negotiate with foreign governments, it gives Congress authority to regulate international trade. TPA allows the Congress to show leadership on trade policy by doing three important things: (1) It allows Congress to set negotiating objectives for new trade pacts; (2) it requires the executive branch to consult extensively with Congress during negotiations; and (3) it gives Congress the final say on any trade agreement in the form of an up-or-down vote. The result is a true partnership stretching the length of Pennsylvania Avenue.

If we fail to renew TPA, U.S. workers and companies will be left at a sharp disadvantage. To oppose TPA is to guarantee that foreign markets remain closed to U.S. exports. To reject TPA is to accept a playing field skewed against American workers and companies.

Congress has granted every president from Franklin D. Roosevelt to George W. Bush the authority to negotiate market-opening trade agreements in consultation with Congress. However, TPA lapsed in 2007. That is unacceptable; every American president should have TPA.

Conclusion

For the Chamber, the agenda is clear. The United States cannot afford to sit on the sidelines while others design a new architecture for the world economy and world trade.

A comprehensive, ambitious, and enforceable market-opening TPP has the potential to create a dramatic increase in trade, spurring economic growth and the creation of American jobs. It would also demonstrate continued U.S. engagement and leadership across the region. It is an exciting vision which, on the right terms, can be an economic shot in the arm for the United States and for our friends and allies in the region. It can send a clear, unmistakable message that America's leadership in the Pacific is here to stay.

At stake is the standing of the United States as the world's leading power, our ability to exert positive influence around the world, our reputation and brand overseas, and our best hopes for dynamic economic growth and job creation. The U.S. Chamber of Commerce looks forward to working with the members of the Committee to secure a commercially strong TPP agreement as soon as possible.

Mr. SALMON. Thank you.
Mr. Miller?

STATEMENT OF MR. SCOTT MILLER, SENIOR ADVISER AND WILLIAM M. SCHOLL CHAIR IN INTERNATIONAL BUSINESS, CENTER FOR STRATEGIC AND INTERNATIONAL STUDIES

Mr. MILLER. Thank you, Mr. Chairman and Mr. Ranking Member, for the opportunity to present my thoughts on prospects for the TPP.

I believe a completed TPP would be beneficial to U.S. interests. First, it would form the largest free trade area in which the U.S. participates with the opportunity to expand its membership. Second, it would establish a modern set of commercial rules for the Asia Pacific where U.S. firms have a large and growing interest. Third, it would reinforce U.S. presence in the region. It is an important economic complement to our security posture.

The United States has compelling economic interest in the Asia Pacific. The Asia Pacific as defined by the 21 APEC economies would be home to three largest economies in the world—the United States, China and Japan. In addition, there are 15 economies worldwide with over $1 trillion of gross domestic product. Eight of those fifteen are APEC members.

This is an area that which over the past decade or two has demonstrated very strong economic growth and relative stability. Among the 21 APEC economies there is already a high level of economic integration. There are many regional trading arrangements of which the United States is a party to a few of them, but there is about $10 trillion a year in goods and services traded around the Asia Pacific.

TPP holds the promise of three major benefits to the U.S. economy—modernized rules, improved market access and a durable new commercial architecture in this fast-growing region. Let me focus in particular on the rules because it came up in your opening comments.

Mr. Chairman, you mentioned globalization and the fact that this economic change is a given in our lives. I think the point that I would make is over time trade rules made for a different time become either outmoded or incomplete for changes wrought by this technology. We certainly live in a time of great technological progress. The technological progress particularly in transportation, communication and information flows have led to rapidly falling barriers in the flow of goods, people, ideas and culture.

It is something, globalization is the usual way to refer to it, but this technological change has changed both the way we trade and what we trade. How has it changed the way we trade? Well, 50 years ago when the GATT was founded and shortly after, most international exchange took in the form of arms length transactions between unrelated parties. What technology allows today, particularly communication and information technology, is a very high degree of firm to firm coordination in trade. The UNCTAD estimates that 80 percent of global merchandise trade is actually firm directed, so the unrelated party transactions that were the basis of the GATT are no longer the reality of modern trade.

So how we trade today and the way we operate is organized around the global value chains and firm communication, so it is a very different mode of operation.

In addition, what we trade has changed because of technology. Some goods and services previously thought non-tradeable including, say, accounting services, are now in fact tradeable goods. More importantly, there are goods that frankly didn't exist 20 years ago when the last round of the GATT was completed that are now in the traded system.

A good example is digital services. In 1994, there was essentially no commercial use of the Internet. At that time digital trade exports or digital services exports from the United States were insignificant. Today, digital services exports are roughly double agricultural exports for the United States. In 2011, digital services exports were $356 billion versus $136 billion of total farm exports.

So we have types of trade today that were unimagined even at the time of the last GATT round. Modernizing rules in areas like cross-border data flows and regulatory cooperation are critical to the way the modern trading system functions. That is really one of the important reasons for being at the table in TPP. They are vital to the U.S. firms which are often on the leading edge of this commercial innovation. As Tami mentioned, TPP will also improve market access for U.S. exporters particularly in the five partner economies where we do not have FTAs now.

And finally, TPP is intended to have an open architecture expected to incorporate new members which will help reinforce U.S. high standards for commerce in the region and have positive spill-over effects for the United States, our allies and our partners in the region.

I thank you for your attention and I look forward to your questions. Thank you.

[The prepared statement of Mr. Miller follows:]

CSIS | CENTER FOR STRATEGIC & INTERNATIONAL STUDIES

Statement before the House Committee on Foreign Affairs

Subcommittee on Asia and the Pacific

"THE TRANS-PACIFIC PARTNERSHIP: PROSPECTS FOR GREATER U.S.TRADE"

A Statement by:

Scott Miller

William M. Scholl Chair in International Business

Center for Strategic and International Studies (CSIS)

March 4, 2015

2172 Rayburn House Office Building

WWW.CSIS.ORG   1616 RHODE ISLAND AVENUE NW. | TEL. (202) 887.0200
WASHINGTON, DC 20036 | FAX (202) 775.3199

Miller: HFAC Asia Pacific Subcommittee   March 4, 2015

Introduction

Mr. Chairman, Mr. Ranking Member, Members of the Subcommittee, thank you for this opportunity to offer my thoughts on the prospects for the Trans-Pacific Partnership (TPP).

TPP is a regional trade agreement that the United States is negotiating with 11 other Asia-Pacific economies (Australia, Brunei, Canada, Chile, Japan, Malaysia, Mexico, New Zealand, Peru, Singapore, and Vietnam). The goal of the negotiations is to produce a comprehensive, high-standard agreement that supports economic growth and addresses twenty-first century trade issues. The office of the U.S. Trade Representative is leading the negotiations for the United States, and has been consulting with Congress and private sector stakeholders at all stages of the negotiations.

A completed TPP would create the largest free-trade area in which the U.S. participates, representing 40 percent of all U.S. merchandise trade, with potential for expansion to other regional economies. TPP would establish a modern set of commercial rules for the Asia-Pacific, where U.S. firms have a large and growing stake. Further, TPP reinforces U.S. presence in the region, "embedding" the United States as a Pacific power.

TPP negotiations are now nearing the end of a long arc. The George W. Bush administration joined the P-4 (Singapore, Brunei, Chile, and New Zealand) in 2008 to launch TPP. The Obama administration embraced the initiative in early 2010, which helped expand the deal to its current 12 parties. Talks are now nearing completion: during the Asia-Pacific Economic Cooperation (APEC) meetings in November 2014, leaders stated, "with the end coming into focus, we have instructed our Ministers to make concluding this agreement a top priority."[1]

Commercial Importance of the Asia-Pacific

The United States has compelling economic interests in the Asia-Pacific. In 2014, the 21 member economies of the Asia-Pacific Economic Cooperation (APEC) grouping, which includes the United States, accounted for 58 percent of global gross domestic product (GDP).[2] The region is home to the world's three largest economies by GDP – the United States, China, and Japan – and 8 of its 15 economies with GDP in excess of $1 trillion/year. The Asia-Pacific is home to fast-growing, relatively stable economies: the International Monetary Fund (IMF) projects that emerging and developing Asia will grow 6.4 percent in 2015, consistent with its growth rates for

---

[1] Leaders' Statement, 2014 APEC Leaders Meeting, Beijing

[2] White House Office of the Press Secretary, "Fact Sheet: 22nd Annual APEC Economic Leaders' Meeting," November 11, 2014, http://www.whitehouse.gov/the-press-office/2014/11/11/fact-sheet-2nd-annual-apec-economic-leaders-meeting.

over a decade.[3] By 2030, it is expected that Asia will be home to over three billion middle-class consumers.[4]

These trends will likely boost the already high levels of economic integration in the region. Last year, more than $10 trillion in goods and services flowed around the Pacific, and the APEC region accounted for 44 percent of total global trade.[5] Six of America's top 10 trading partners are in APEC, and U.S. exports to APEC member economies have more than doubled over the past decade. Continued growth in the Asia-Pacific will lead to even greater demand for high-quality U.S. goods and services.

Economic growth in the Asia-Pacific translates to jobs at home. The International Trade Administration estimates that exports to Asia and the Pacific supported 3.2 million jobs across the United States in 2013, the largest share of any single region.[6] That same year, Asian companies with investments in the United States directly employed nearly one million Americans, with many more jobs supported indirectly by these operations.[7]

Core Benefits of TPP

The Trans-Pacific Partnership is expected to deliver three critically-important benefits to the U.S. economy: modernized rules, improved market access opportunities for U.S. exporters, and a durable new commercial architecture for economies in the Asia-Pacific.

First, TPP intends to address an array of new issues for which existing trade rules are incomplete or outmoded. Technological progress in information, communication, and transportation, where American innovators frequently play a leading role, has dramatically changed the nature of international trade and investment. Often referred to as "globalization," these technological advances have led to rapidly-falling barriers to the movement of goods, people, ideas, and culture, as well as a concurrent rise in inter-country competitiveness. Firms now have the ability to coordinate tasks across broad geographies, and at the same time technology has expanded the range of tradable goods and services. Production now

---

[3] International Monetary Fund, "January Update: Cross Currents," *World Economic Outlook,* January 2015, https://www.imf.org/external/pubs/ft/weo/2015/update/01/.
[4] Dominic Wilson and Raluca Dragusanu, "The Expanding Middle: The Exploding World Middle Class and Falling Global Inequality," Goldman Sachs, Global Economics Paper #170, July 7, 2008. https://360.gs.com
[5] White House Office of the Press Secretary, *op cit.*
[6] Chris Rasmussen and Elizabeth Schaefer, "Jobs Supported by Export Destination 2013," International Trade Administration, U.S. Department of Commerce, July 7, 2014, http://www.trade.gov/mas/ian/build/groups/public/@tg_ian/documents/webcontent/tg_ian_0053 72.pdf.
[7] Organization for International Investment, "Insourcing Facts," August 2012, http://www.ofii.org/resources/insourcing-facts. Estimate based on Asia's share of overall U.S. inbound FDI.

takes place in "global value chains," with goods being "made in the world" rather than originating from a single economy.[8]

The rules-based trading system established by the GATT has helped to advance prosperity and peace, but the underlying idea of the GATT – regulating arm's-length transactions between unrelated parties – no longer represents the bulk of trade and investment flows. UNCTAD estimates that over 80 percent of merchandise trade is firm-directed.[9] For the United States, trade rules and the negotiations that define them need to keep pace with the speed of innovation, and TPP seeks to modernize the rules to better reflect the changed trading environment.

Since the conclusion of GATT 1994, the most recent multilateral agreement, technological progress has changed not just how we trade, but what we trade. Goods and services previously considered non-tradable, or which did not exist at all, are now a part of global commerce. Digital services are a good example. At the time GATT 1994 entered into force, there was essentially no commercial use of the internet, and digital services exports were insignificant. Since then, digital services have grown to become a major factor in U.S. export performance: the U.S. International Trade Commission estimates that U.S. exports of digital services in 2011 totaled $356 billion, more than double the $136 billion of U.S. agricultural exports that same year.[10]

TPP negotiators are working to modernize the "rules of the road" for emerging issues like cross-border data flows, regulatory cooperation, and competitive neutrality for state-owned enterprises. Importantly, because six parties already have FTAs with the United States, TPP represents the best way to update existing U.S. FTAs to better reflect current commercial practices and allow the United States to maximize the gains of commercial innovation.

Second, TPP will expand U.S. trade and investment opportunities. This is especially the case in the five economies that are not currently U.S. FTA partners, including Japan, the world's third largest economy. In 2013, the U.S. exported $87.0 billion in goods and $51.1 billion in services to these five "new FTA" partners. Improved market access achieved in the TPP negotiations holds the promise of substantial economic gains from this strong base. The Peterson Institute for International Economics has estimated $223.4 billion in annual global welfare gains from a concluded TPP in 2025, including $76.6 billion in GDP gains for the United

---

[8] For a more complete description of this process, see OECD (2013), "Interconnected Economies: Benefiting from Global Value Chains," OECD Publishing,
http://www.oecd.org/sti/ind/interconnected-economies-GVCs-synthesis.pdf
[9] UNCTAD (2013) "World Investment Report: Global Value Chains, Investment, and Trade for Development," EISBN 978-92-1-056212-6
[10] USITC (2014) "Digital Trade in the United States and Global Economies, Part Two," Publication no. 4485, Investigation no. 332-540.

States and a $123.5 billion increase in U.S. exports relative to the baseline scenario.[11]

Third, TPP is intended to have "open architecture," which will allow it to incorporate new members after its conclusion. This strengthens its potential as a driver and *de facto* template for a new system of rules. A new high-standard regime would have positive effects for U.S. economic and commercial interests, positive spillover effects for our allies and partners in the region, and create new incentives for countries to seek to upgrade their own standards.

TPP would embed the United States more deeply in the Asia-Pacific region and reinvigorate American leadership there. It would strengthen trade and investment ties across the Pacific and deepen regional economic integration. It would also demonstrate a long-term American commitment to the region that complements our security presence there. Our Asian partners want the U.S. military to remain in the region, but they do not want only that; they also seek our markets, capital, ideas, and leadership in advancing economic rules of the road.

The Obama administration has invested substantial prestige in a successful conclusion of TPP. Concluding and ratifying TPP is not just central to the administration's regional economic policy but also the entire Asia rebalancing strategy, as a complement to the U.S. security and diplomatic presence in the region.

Conclusion

TPP is at the core of U.S. economic strategy in the Asia Pacific. A successful conclusion will promote economic growth at home, and help modernize and advance an open, rules-based trading system which has long been central to U.S. interests. And TPP will advance a commercial architecture which embeds American presence in the Asia-Pacific, continuing the longstanding U.S. commitment to the region's security and prosperity.

Thank you for your attention.

---

[11] From Peter A. Petri, Michael G. Plummer, Fan Zhai, *The Trans-Pacific Partnership and Asia-Pacific Integration: A Quantitative Assessment*, Peterson Institute for International Economics and East West Center, Updated May, 2013, http://asiapacifictrade.org/wp-content/uploads/2013/05/Adding-Japan-and-Korea-to-TPP.pdf.

Mr. SALMON. Thank you.
Ms. Drake?

STATEMENT OF MS. CELESTE DRAKE, TRADE AND GLOBALIZATION POLICY SPECIALIST, THE AMERICAN FEDERATION OF LABOR AND CONGRESS OF INDUSTRIAL ORGANIZATIONS

Ms. DRAKE. Thank you. Chairman Salmon, Ranking Member Sherman, members of the committee, good afternoon. I appreciate this opportunity to testify in the prospects for greater trade under the proposed Trans-Pacific Partnership. I have submitted written testimony for the record and will summarize my comments here.

I am going to start with the premise that some of you might find surprising, and that is that American workers support trade and in fact we want more of it. While it is true that we oppose the recent Colombia and Korea trade deals, it is also true that we strongly support GSP and AGOA which promote imports through tariff reductions.

For us, the real question is not whether to trade but how to trade. In other words, what rules will govern and who benefits? Some say the TPP is a fight between the U.S. and China to write trade rules. It is not that simple. Is the ''we'' really the people of the United States, writ large, or is it global corporations, many of whom invest in and produce in China, and other economic elites who hold about 90 percent of the U.S. trade advisor seats? For China, a real problem is getting it to abide by any rules. Fourteen years after China joined the WTO it is still not compliant and why would new rules be any different?

For the nearly 13 million working families the AFL–CIO represents, the question we ask is whether taken as a whole the Trans-Pacific Partnership will make lives better for people who work. There is little doubt that a completed TPP will increase trade flows, which do not necessarily mean better lives for workers. Better wages and working conditions do. Trade rules from NAFTA onward have contributed to stagnant wages and increasing inequality.

How can a trade deal help? The most important thing the TPP can do to help create jobs and raise wages is to address currency manipulation. A Japanese official recently warned that such a move would kill the TPP. But we have real doubts about the value of a TPP that fails to address currency. This is critical. If the TPP leaves countries free to use currency to create trade advantages, the mammoth, job-killing $500 billion U.S. trade deficit is only likely to grow.

We are also looking for commercial rules that will help reduce the deficit. This means strong rules of origin on everything from cars and car parts to aerospace parts and clothing. It also means meaningful, easy-to-use rules to prevent unfair competition from government subsidized firms that compete against our firms, for instance, by producing steel products. It also means intellectual property provisions that strongly support American innovation and creativity without putting health at risk or bleeding taxpayers dry.

We support balanced investment rules, not investor to state dispute settlement. ISDS sets up a separate but unequal system of justice that operates outside U.S. courts and U.S. law available to foreign investors only. This corporate court undermines the ability of elected officials to make policy choices.

And though the quality of a trade deal does not turn solely on labor provisions, inadequate standards, poor enforcement or both contribute to an economic imbalance that leaves workers behind. The TPP's labor rules must require compliance on day one or it sends the message that the commitments aren't serious. If the TPP's labor rules are entirely discretionary, allow for infinite delays or no action at all, they will not help workers gain the voice they need to raise wages and make their jobs safer.

The GAO has already recognized inadequate U.S. oversight and monitoring of labor provisions in prior trade deals, even ones using the so-called May 10th Standard. Workers, whether in Mesa, Arizona, Mexico City or Hanoi, cannot afford to have their governments ignore fundamental human rights, including the right to join together and seek a better life.

Some of the TPP countries are extremely troublesome in this regard whether that means restricting the right to free speech, to join a union, arresting people who wear Santa hats or stoning homosexuals, all of these raise concerns about the ability of these countries to be fair trading partners, to meet international standards and to develop an economy with the basic fairness to create a functioning middle class.

These are human rights questions, moral questions, but also deeply economic questions. To us, the questions about the TPP are far too complex to merit a grant of Fast Track which requires Congress to commit sight unseen to an up or down vote with limited debate. That is why we urge you to increase your leverage over the TPP by rejecting the unaccountable Fast Track model. We cannot afford to get this wrong.

I thank the committee for its time and would be pleased to answer any questions you may have.

[The prepared statement of Ms. Drake follows:]

American Federation of Labor and Congress of Industrial Organizations

815 Sixteenth Street, N.W.
Washington, D.C. 20006
(202) 637-5000
www.aflcio.org

BEFORE THE HOUSE
SUBCOMMITTEE ON ASIA AND THE PACIFIC
OF THE COMMITTEE ON FOREIGN AFFAIRS

HEARING ON

"THE TRANS-PACIFIC PARTNERSHIP: PROSPECTS FOR GREATER U.S. TRADE"

TESTIMONY OF

CELESTE DRAKE
AMERICAN FEDERATION OF LABOR &
CONGRESS OF INDUSTRIAL ORGANIZATIONS (AFL-CIO)

MARCH 4, 2015

Distinguished members of the Foreign Affairs Subcommittee on Asia and the Pacific, it is an honor to testify on the Trans-Pacific Partnership and prospects for greater trade on behalf of the American Federation of Labor and Congress of Industrial Organizations (AFL-CIO), its affiliate unions, and nearly 13 million working men and women in all fifty states. The AFL-CIO has long recognized that workers everywhere live in a global economic environment. Trade and globalization are not a temporary trend; they are an economic reality. The key question is how to shape these forces so that they help build shared prosperity and sustainable growth. It is critical that the U.S. approach couples expansion and enforcement of labor rights globally with necessary reforms in trade and domestic economic policy, as well as market opening measures.

America's working families have good reason to be suspicious of our current trade regime, which has contributed to the closure of 60,000 factories, record trade deficits, net job losses in the millions, and stagnating and even falling wages. Current U.S. trade deals, which began with NAFTA and continued with the Korea and Colombia agreements, among others, undermine shared prosperity by encouraging employers to pit one group of workers against another—both within and between countries. Under this model, our trade deficit has increased dramatically—from $70 billion in 1993, the year before NAFTA went into effect, to more than $505 billion today (in nominal terms). It has also contributed to the decoupling of wages and productivity, meaning as U.S. workers are more productive, they fail to reap the gains of that productivity in their wages.

The rules first enshrined in NAFTA accelerate and reward outsourcing by providing extraordinary protections for foreign investors and intellectual property rights and locking in market access, while leaving workers' rights and environmental protections vulnerable. While there have been some improvements in the trade template in the decades since NAFTA, unfortunately they have been inadequate to reverse this dynamic. Taken together, our trade agreements continue to promote a race to the bottom, undermining the legal and regulatory framework that made the American economy the envy of the world, including in terms of workers' rights, wages, pensions, and working conditions.

We need an entirely new framework, not mere tinkering around the edges, to ensure that these trade deals contribute to good jobs, sustainable growth, and a healthy environment. Unfortunately, too many advocates for the TPP present the choices facing America's future in unhelpful ways. For instance, the choice is not the TPP as currently conceived versus no international trade at all. Neither is it America versus China. The correct frame for these choices is "How do we structure international trade rules so that they promote good, family-wage jobs, sustainable growth, dynamic economies, smart natural resource conservation, and the realization of human rights and dignity globally?"

These are weighty and complicated choices facing us as a society—and they are unlikely to be best resolved by limiting Congressional oversight, input, and debate into trade policies that last, potentially, forever. The debate is not advanced by posing the question in nationalist terms, nor by simplistic black-and-white scenarios, nor by setting up artificial walls between consideration of domestic and international economic policies. America's workers will not reap a fair share of the benefits of trade if we fail to ensure we have broad economic policies that support workers and businesses alike. These include, for instance,

- o Enacting currency legislation that ensures the administration can treat currency manipulation as a countervailable duty;
- o Enacting expanded and enhanced skills training for all workers, not just those whose jobs have been displaced by trade;
- o Increasing federal funding to upgrade and rebuild ports, airports, railroads, roads, schools, water systems and other critical public infrastructure so that the United States does not lose private investment due to old and crumbling public facilities;
- o Strengthening trade enforcement and remedies;
- o Ensuring that the Export-Import Bank and other export support programs do what they are supposed to do: support U.S. exports and jobs;
- o Strengthening "Buy America" and "Buy American" laws; and
- o Strengthening domestic laws that protect the fundamental human rights to associate freely and engage in collective bargaining.

The AFL-CIO urges Congress to consider and pass legislation addressing these important issues *before* considering new trade agreements such as the Trans-Pacific Partnership. Only when appropriate domestic policies are in place will the American economy be able to take full advantage of any growth opportunities created by expanded trade.

We are concerned that if Congress and the administration embark on a "TPP first" path instead of a "jobs first" path, the opportunities for workers—both in the U.S. and globally—will be squandered. The effects of failing to put in place proper domestic economic policies, of course, will be exacerbated by a TPP that enables global firms to use the United States as a flag of convenience. It simply is not the case that the national interest is entirely coincident with the interest of such firms, many of which have increased profits by pitting countries against one another in the quest to attract foreign investment by reducing costs related to maintaining labor, environmental and social standards. This is fundamentally at odds with the economic interests of the United States and its citizens, and in many cases also at odds with the interests of our trading partners, who seek rising living standards in their own countries.

While we know that market opening can be beneficial, we also know that the TPP, and the kind of privileges it appears set to provide to global firms, in many cases have little to do with market opening. Instead, many of these policies are about providing extraordinary legal privileges to foreign-invested firms, granting additional monopoly rights to makers of life-saving medicines, creating tools designed to undermine differences in consumer protection policies, and the like. The AFL-CIO recommends that Congress and the American people engage in a full and frank discussion of these issues, rather than glossing over them by declaring the TPP simply a market opening measure.

Key among the questions for Congress in its evaluation of the benefits for the TPP for the American and global economy are the following:

Currency: Addressing currency misalignment is probably the single action the U.S. can take that will have the biggest impact on jobs. The fact that currency provisions continue to be absent from the TPP is disturbing on two fronts: it is a both glaring policy omission and a procedural concern. In the absence of existing Fast Track legislation, one trade-related issue on which bipartisan majorities of the House and Senate have spoken while the TPP has been under negotiation is currency.

Misaligned currency is an important contributing factor to the U.S. trade imbalance with China and other Asian nations. The Peterson Institute for International Economics cited Japan, Malaysia, and Singapore as "egregious" currency manipulators in 2012. [1] The Economic Policy Institute estimates the U.S. could add as many as 5.8 million jobs by eliminating such currency manipulation.[2]

Without effective currency disciplines, a TPP country could freely undermine the price-reduction effects of tariff elimination overnight by manipulating its currency, making its goods artificially less expensive than ours and exacerbating our $500 billion trade deficit. The justification for the administration's omission (that our own monetary policy practices could be challenged) is a distraction: central banks engaging in monetary policy are not the problem, sustained interventions in currency markets in order to create and maintain trade surpluses are.[3] Various workable proposals have been put forward to address this concern, including using guidelines already established by the International Monetary Fund (IMF). American automobile producers have also put forth a proposal.[4]

The failure to include mandatory currency manipulation provisions subject to dispute settlement in the TPP leaves working families behind. Moreover, it undercuts the argument that the TPP will allow the U.S., rather than China, to "write the rules" of trade for the Pacific region. Continuing the current approach to currency market intervention allows China, and the U.S. firms that export from there, to continue to "write the rules" in ways detrimental to U.S.-based producers and their employees. Congress should examine whether omitting enforceable currency rules from the TPP is the correct approach, and whether the TPP will live up to its promises given this conspicuous omission.

Investment: To ensure that the TPP achieves shared prosperity, it should provide better balance in its investment provisions. Dozens of labor, environmental organizations, faith groups, business groups, farm groups, consumer groups, and poverty reduction groups have called for the elimination of the special legal rules and private tribunals for foreign investors known as investor-to-state dispute settlement (ISDS). ISDS is a key tool in undermining democratic

---

[1] *See, e.g.,* Joseph E. Gagnon, "Combating Widespread Currency Manipulation," PIIE Policy Brief No. PB12-19, July 2012, available at: http://www.piie.com/publications/pb/pb12-19.pdf.

[2] *See* Robert E. Scott, "Stop Currency Manipulation and Create Millions of Jobs," Economic Policy Institute, February 26, 2014, available at: http://www.epi.org/publication/stop-currency-manipulation-and-create-millions-of-jobs/.

[3] Rep. Sander Levin, TPP in Focus: The need to address currency manipulation in TPP, and why U.S. monetary policy is not at risk, Ways and Means Committee Democrats website, Feb. 6, 2015, available here: http://democrats.waysandmeans.house.gov/blog/tpp-focus-need-address-currency-manipulation-tpp-and-why-us-monetary-policy-not-risk.

[4] The proposal can be found here: http://www.americanautocouncil.org/tpp.

control over corporate excesses, and is currently being used to attack public health policies in Australia and Uruguay, environmental policies in Canada and Peru, and labor provisions in Egypt.

Rather than challenge actual takings or discriminatory policies, global firms use ISDS to seek compensation for "regulatory takings," a discredited concept not applicable under U.S. law. Instead of promoting a global regulatory takings regime that privatizes the gains of foreign investment while socializing its losses, the TPP can achieve reasonable protections for investors through state-to-state dispute settlement as well as development assistance targeted toward building and maintaining rule of law in our trading partner countries. Firms seeking additional protections should buy political risk insurance policies.[5] The option to negotiate alternative dispute provisions in investment contracts with host governments presents yet another opportunity for firms seeking to minimize risk.

No credible evidence has been marshalled to show that ISDS provisions solve measurable real world problems or are conclusively linked to increased investment. Rather, ISDS provisions in the TPP pose a threat to democratic decision making, particularly at the state and local level. For our trading partners, some of whose GDPs are dwarfed by the annual income of the world's largest firms, ISDS can pose an even bigger threat. At the extreme, it can interfere with the development of modern, reliable, regulatory and judicial systems—the kind that make life better and more stable for businesses, workers, and consumers.

We urge Congress to reconsider, particularly in consultation with state and local officials, the wisdom of opening the U.S. to additional challenges by Japanese, Australian, Malaysian, and other firms.

Climate: Currently, U.S. trade policy could undermine both domestic efforts to address climate and the administration's bilateral agreement with China to cooperate on climate change and clean energy. Unless the TPP sets the bar in line with the recent bilateral agreement with China, it represents a missed opportunity.[6]

Moreover, if the U.S. were to impose strict emission standards, a broad based carbon tax, a carbon cap and trade scheme, or virtually any concrete but unilateral policy designed to reduce polluting emissions, such policies could of course induce some firms to consider moving production outside the U.S.—undermining our economic growth as well as emissions control

---

[5] The Cato Institute has written convincingly about how ISDS undermines free market principles. *See, e.g.,* Simon Lester, *Responding to the White House Response on ISDS*, Feb. 27, 2015, available here: http://www.cato.org/blog/responding-white-house-defense-investor-state-dispute-settlement; and Daniel J. Ikenson, *A Compromise to Advance the Trade Agenda: Purge Negotiations of Investor-State Dispute Settlement*, Mar. 4, 2014 available here: http://www.cato.org/publications/free-trade-bulletin/compromise-advance-trade-agenda-purge-negotiations-investor-state.

[6] See FACT SHEET: U.S.-China Joint Announcement on Climate Change and Clean Energy Cooperation, available at: http://www.whitehouse.gov/the-press-office/2014/11/11/fact-sheet-us-china-joint-announcement-climate-change-and-clean-energy-c.

efforts. Without a border adjustment—to adjust the cost of highly polluting imports so that clean U.S. and dirty foreign goods could fairly compete—the TPP will do nothing to stop manufacturers from closing up shop in the U.S. and moving to TPP countries with no carbon reduction scheme in order to sell cheaper, dirtier goods here and around the globe, undercutting not only our workers but our efforts to slow climate change.

It is not known whether the TPP now contains effective and enforceable climate measures, a border adjustment mechanism, or related policies that would prevent undercutting of national efforts to transition to a cleaner, greener economy. It should.

While it may be true that the U.S. can unilaterally impose a border adjustment measure at any time and does not need a trade deal to do so, doing nothing in the TPP to bring other countries along as part of a just transition to a cleaner economy fails to show leadership and leaves the playing field tilted against U.S. workers and responsible climate policy. To set the stage for future action, it would be better if U.S. trade and energy policy were in harmony, so that U.S. lawmakers could have greater confidence that any conservation efforts they might consider would not harm our competitiveness. To set the 21st Century standard TPP backers have promised, the TPP must address climate threats in a responsible way and ensure that U.S. efforts to limit carbon emissions do not backfire on our own workers or on the future of the planet.

Labor: The labor movement has been clear from the outset of the TPP talks that the status quo on labor (the so-called "May 10" agreement) was not good enough. The "May 10" standards (created as bipartisan compromise between the Republican Bush Administration and Democratic leaders in the House) represented a step forward from CAFTA, but were never sufficient to truly level the playing field for workers inside and outside the U.S. or to remedy the weakness of the virtually unfettered discretion that the U.S. and trading partner nations enjoy to delay or ignore labor rights submissions indefinitely. In 2011, the AFL-CIO joined with labor federations from the majority of TPP countries to draft and submit a comprehensive labor chapter that attempted to address past shortcomings. However, given the secrecy of TPP negotiations, we cannot say whether what will emerge in the final TPP will be able to reasonably be called a meaningful improvement over "May 10."

As the AFL-CIO has previously noted, the choice of trading partners in the TPP is cause for great concern: barring a decades-long delay between the Administration's slated completion date for the TPP and its entry into force, we foresee virtually no possibility that Vietnam will be in compliance with even "May 10" labor commitments on day one. Despite a reported willingness to engage with the U.S. government on labor issues, it is difficult to imagine the single party Government of Vietnam instituting the legal, regulatory, and enforcement changes necessary to fully respect the right of free association necessary for the effective functioning of representative worker organizations. As recently as last September, a senior economic adviser for the general secretary of Vietnam's Communist Party indicated that labor issues remain the biggest obstacle for Vietnam. He told the Voice of America "there has been no sign that Hanoi will compromise on the issues of human rights, labor rights and independent trade unions."[7]

---

[7] "Vietnam Rights Still Obstacle to TPP Membership," *Voice of America News*, Sept. 11, 2014, available at: http://www.voanews.com/content/vietnam-rights-still-an-obstacle-to-tpp-membership/2446966.html.

Moreover, as explained in a recent AFL-CIO publication,[8] at least three other TPP partners, namely Malaysia, Brunei, and Mexico, have human rights shortcomings so serious as to require major shifts in labor policy and enforcement to come into compliance with internationally recognized labor rights on day one.

To let the TPP enter into force without full compliance with all labor commitments from all twelve countries could undermine the entire agreement. It sends that message that promises to comply—in any area—are sufficient. If the TPP is going to have beneficial effects, promises and changes on paper are not enough. Nor do they reset the playing field in ways beneficial for workers in the U.S. or globally.

The issue of labor rights compliance is critical. It creates the space necessary for workers, both in the U.S. and in our TPP partner countries, to engage in the give and take necessary to raise their pay, benefits, and conditions of work. If workers lack the basic rights to speak up about workplace conditions and to join together in common cause to improve their lot, it simply exacerbates—rather than improves—the status quo, which has been used to keep wages lower than they might otherwise be both in the U.S. and globally. This is causing a global weakness in demand that hampers growth and exacerbates inequality. The IMF even recognizes this link between a lack of unions and an increase in inequality.[9] Trade policy that concentrates wealth in the hand of a few by failing to adequately promote workplace rights fails workers—no matter where they reside.

Without high labor and human rights standards and strong enforcement tools that cannot be weakened through delay, inaction, or the acceptance of "progress" as a substitute for real improvements, the labor chapter of the TPP will continue to erode bargaining power of workers both here and abroad, facilitating rather than combatting the race to the bottom.

State-Owned Enterprises: The AFL-CIO continues to be concerned about the ability of the TPP to adequately protect against unfair competition by state-sponsored and state-supported companies with respect to investments on American soil that would compete head-to-head with existing non-state sponsored companies here at home.

Government Procurement: The AFL-CIO has long opposed procurement chapters altogether. We believe that government procurement at the federal, state, and local level is an important job creation tool that should not be blunted by commitments to foreign firms. The AFL-CIO strongly supports the widest possible use of Buy American and Buy "State" policies as well as ensuring that bidding specifications and criteria can include good governance policies such as "clean hands" and preferences to firms with better safety and job performance records.

Rules of Origin: We remain concerned that the rules of origin for the TPP may not be effective at preventing "leakage." When TPP advocates claim that the TPP will ensure that the U.S. "writes the rules" instead of China, Congress should ask whether China will in fact be able to

---

[8] *See* Annex.

[9] Florence Jaumotte and Carolina Osorio Buitron, "Power from the People," *Finance & Development*, Vol. 52, No. 1, International Monetary Fund, March 2015, available at: http://www.imf.org/external/pubs/ft/fandd/2015/03/jaumotte.htm.

benefit greatly from the TPP without ever joining. Weak rules of origin will promote greater use of Chinese inputs, which can be made in contravention of TPP rules, into finished products that then become eligible for TPP benefits.

Public Services: To ensure that the American people retain the right to determine the quantity, quality, type, and nature of public services offered by the federal, as well as local and states governments the AFL-CIO has recommended a broad carve-out from the services commitments for important public services. At this point, there are no indications that the agreement will change the commitments from prior agreements such as the WTO and the Colombia FTA, which fail to adequately protecting the right to provide and regulate public services in a manner consistent with the desires of voters. The key question is not the straw man of forced privatization. Instead, the question is whether governments retain the right to freely—that is, without compensating foreign firms or trading partners—reverse failed privatization efforts. This question becomes even more salient as evaluators, such as the non-profit, non-partisan Project on Government Oversight, compile compelling data on privatization efforts that actually decrease the value that America's taxpayers get for their dollar.[10]

Financial Services: The AFL-CIO has recommended changes to both the "prudential exception" and the restriction on capital controls (the latter consistent with the latest IMF guidance) from the terms used in prior trade agreements, to ensure countries can act, free from the deterring effect of even frivolous claims, to stabilize their economies and protect themselves from financial crises. Malaysia effectively used capital control measures in the late 1990s to protect itself from the worst of the Asian financial crisis. We recommend that Congress thoroughly and deliberately consider whether the TPP will safeguard against another global financial meltdown, or whether it will increase the likelihood of one by deterring our trading partners from acting boldly in the face of an impending crisis.

Access to Medicines: The AFL-CIO has recommended that the U.S. exclude TRIPS-plus provisions from the TPP, and barring that, we recommended that the U.S. preserve the "May 10" provisions on medicines. We also recommended the omission of provisions modeled after those in the U.S.-Korea-FTA that can interfere with efforts to keep government spending on drugs and devices in check. Quality, affordable, accessible healthcare is not only a human right—it enhances worker attendance and productivity. Trade policy should not interfere with public choices about how best to make healthcare available to a nation's residents, nor should it impinge on development and humanitarian assistance by artificially making such assistance more expensive. Congress, therefore, should consider carefully whether the rules of the TPP promote or impede domestic healthcare policy as well as global human development efforts.

Indeed, the TPP may be too complex to stake out a position "for" or "against" without careful consideration of its voluminous text, a careful study of the impacts of prior, similarly structured

---

[10] In 2011, the Project on Government Oversight (POGO) compared the costs of federal employees and contractors in a seminal study entitled *Bad Business: Billions of Taxpayer Dollars Wasted on Hiring Contractors*, the first to compare service contractor billing rates to the salaries and benefits of federal employees. POGO determined that "on average, contractors charge the government almost twice as much as the annual compensation of comparable federal employees. Of the 35 types of jobs that POGO looked at in its new report, it was cheaper to hire federal workers in all but just 2 cases." The report is available for download here: http://www.pogo.org/our-work/reports/2011/co-gp-20110913.html.

agreements, and broad consultations with legal experts from a variety of points of view who have also had an opportunity to study the texts. Such discussion, study, and thorough evaluation seems unlikely given the current level of secrecy surrounding the texts. Moreover, it seems even less likely to occur should Congress accede to Fast Track authority, which will severely limit the time that Congress and outside experts may study the text before a simple up-or-down vote is required. Finally, should Congress decide that, while the TPP contains some beneficial provisions, on balance it presents a risk to the firms, families, and communities of the 435 Congressional districts, Congress may already have lost much of its leverage to force improvements in the deal if it has previously committed itself to an up or down vote on the TPP, sight unseen.

In sum, to get the TPP right, Congress faces consequential choices that, for the good of the country, should not be constrained by the misguided secrecy, speed, and unaccountability of Fast Track. To best safeguard the authority over trade policy enshrined in Congress by the Constitution, the AFL-CIO recommends that you reject the outdated and undemocratic process known as Fast Track and develop instead a new trade negotiating authority for the 21st Century.[11]

---

[11] *See* Time for a New Track: Time for a New Track: What Labor Unions Mean When We Say Trade Policy Must Ensure That Negotiations Are Transparent, Democratic, and Participatory, available at: http://www.aflcio.org/content/download/132311/3551971/TTPFastTrack_TimeForANewTrack.pdf.

Annex

(also available for download at:
http://www.aflcio.org/content/download/150491/3811471/file/TPPreport-NO+BUG.pdf)

The Trans-Pacific Partnership:
Four Countries That Don't Comply With U.S. Trade Law

THE CURRENT MODEL for U.S. free trade agreements (FTAs) is deeply flawed. Since the North American Free Trade Agreement (NAFTA), FTAs have perpetuated a global race to the bottom, as many countries seek to remain competitive in the global market and maintain low labor costs to attract business by ignoring, or in some cases actively interfering with, fundamental labor rights. Although FTAs contain labor chapters, enforcement of labor laws in partner countries has not been a priority for the U.S. government. The highest labor standards the United States has embedded in FTAs require parties to adopt and implement laws that protect the rights enshrined in the International Labor Organization's (ILO) Declaration on Fundamental Principles and Rights at Work, including freedom of association and collective bargaining.[1] This language was a step forward, despite lacking the specificity and enforceability

of incorporating actual ILO conventions into FTAs. However, the enforcement of these standards has been slow and cumbersome, and relies totally on the political will of governments. Labor provisions, whatever they may be, require active monitoring, investigation and oversight in order to be effective and provide the necessary impetus to comply.

Now the Obama administration wants to Fast Track the largest FTA in history, the Trans-Pacific Partnership (TPP), covering more than 40% of world GDP and about a third of world trade. The TPP would cover the United States and 11 Pacific Rim nations— Australia, Brunei, Canada, Chile, Japan, Malaysia, Mexico, New Zealand, Peru, Singapore and Vietnam. While the specific language of the agreement being negotiated is kept secret, U.S. Trade Representative Michael Froman has promised "groundbreaking" new rules that will bring "new market access for

Made-In-America goods and services, [and] strong and enforceable labor standards and environmental commitments."[2]

The TPP should lead to the creation of decent work and protect the ILO's core labor standards in partner trading countries with effective penalties for violations. However, as at least four of the major countries included in the agreement would be out of compliance on the first day of the TPP, such an outcome appears unlikely.[3] In Mexico, Malaysia, Vietnam and Brunei, workers face ongoing and systemic abuse with either the complicity or direct involvement of the state.

Mexico

The human and labor rights situation in Mexico is deteriorating rapidly. The root causes of the crisis in Mexico are many and complex, including growing economic inequality, unemployment and the absence of decent work, rural displacement since NAFTA, public corruption and the absence of the rule of law. The recent disappearance of 43 students, now declared dead, from the teachers' college in Ayotzinapa, Guerrero, fostered by local police and criminal gangs, is a horrific example of violence, corruption and dissolution of the rule of law. More than 22,000 people have been disappeared since 2007; more than 5,000 vanished in 2014 alone.[4]

These crimes are rarely investigated and almost never prosecuted, allowing public security forces to operate with impunity. Corruption, abuse and impunity also are root causes of the near absence of genuine industrial relations in Mexico, which artificially depresses wages and limits economic growth. Many workers are covered by collective agreements ("protection contracts") they have never seen or ratified through a vote.

Workers who attempt to form independent unions face violence from employers and employer-dominated unions, often in collusion with local authorities. This situation presents itself at the worksites of many multinational companies, including Atento, Excellon, Honda, PKC and Teksid. The persistence of employer-dominated unions is due in part to a system of corrupt labor boards that lack accountability. The ILO has raised serious concerns about the impact of protection contracts on freedom of association. Independent unions and labor experts have proposed mechanisms to address these key problems, including procedures to allow workers to vote on their contracts and the transfer of labor board functions to an independent authority.

In the agricultural sector, violations of fundamental rights occur, as well as widespread displacement. Child labor, forced labor and inhumane working conditions exist on farms that export fresh produce into the United States, which then is sold at major retailers, including Walmart and Safeway.[5] Flawed trade policy that has failed to lift wages or create jobs has driven the displacement of a significant number of rural workers. Mexican workers seeking a better life often are forced to migrate to the United States, where they face further exploitation and criminalization.

These shortcomings are also well documented in the public reports of the U.S. Department of State (DOS) and the International Labor Organization. The problem is not just the weak NAFTA mechanism. It is also the lack of political will to use the weak tools available. The case of Mexico demonstrates the need for broader commitments regarding decent work, labor inspections and constant monitoring of labor conditions to address issues in a timely fashion. It seems unlikely that the TPP will include the high level of commitment needed to address these systemic issues.

Malaysia

Malaysia has grave problems with forced labor and human trafficking. The U.S. Department of Labor (DOL) reports that forced labor is prominent in the electronics, garment and palm oil sectors, which also contain child labor.[6] The majority of the victims of forced labor in Malaysia are among the country's 4 million migrant workers—40% of the overall workforce. Migrants to Malaysia face a range of abuses related to their recruitment and placement, and often are threatened with deportation for speaking out.[7]

Migrant workers in Malaysia generally come from other Asian countries in search of greater opportunities. Often, they encounter forced labor or debt bondage at the hands of their employers, staffing agents or labor recruiters. Migrant workers in the agriculture, construction, textile, electronics and domestic work areas throughout Malaysia are subjected to restrictions on movement, deceit and fraud in wages, document confiscation, and unconscionable debts by recruitment agents or employers. Malaysia currently has the lowest possible ranking—tier 3—on the U.S. Department of State annual Trafficking in Persons report, meaning Malaysia "does not fully comply with the minimum standards [to prevent trafficking] and is not making significant efforts to do so."[8] Migrants also are limited in their ability to improve these conditions, as they are prohibited from engaging in organizing or collective bargaining.

Because of this pervasive exploitation, virtually everyone who regularly uses electronics in the United States has come in contact with forced labor. Some of the most recognizable electronics brands source components from Malaysia, and a recent report from Verité that relied on interviews with more than 500 workers found that approximately 28% of electronics workers toiled in conditions of forced labor. Additionally, 73% of workers reported violations that put them at risk for forced labor, such as outsourcing, debt from recruitment fees, constrained movement, isolation and document retention.[9]

The right to freedom of association and collective bargaining also is regularly violated in Malaysia, contributing to the overall level of exploitation and depressing wages. Collective bargaining is restricted in companies in "pioneer" industries, such as the electronics industry, a highly traded sector, and in the public sector. In eligible industries, the Ministry of Human Resources can refuse to register a trade union without giving any reason and has the power to unilaterally dissolve, suspend or deregister trade union organizations. Freedom of association is strictly limited, as there are many legal restrictions on industrial action, and police permission is required for public gatherings of more than five people.

Vietnam

Vietnam has an authoritarian government that tightly controls political rights, freedom of speech and other civil liberties. The U.S. Department of State reports there is corruption in the judicial system and widespread abuse committed by police and other security forces, including arbitrary killings.[10] The government maintains a prohibition on independent human rights organizations and other civil society groups. Further, the Vietnamese government restricts union activity outside the official unions affiliated

with the Communist Party's Vietnam General Confederation of Labor (VGCL), which actually controls the union registration process.

Wildcat strikes and other industrial actions outside VGCL unions have led to government retaliation where workers have been prosecuted and jailed. Workplace-level VGCL unions generally have management serving in leadership positions, and when that is not the case, workers cannot hold a union meeting without management present.[11] The government blocks access to politically sensitive websites and monitors the internet for the organization of unauthorized demonstrations.[12]

Vietnam has significant problems with forced labor and child labor. The U.S. Department of Labor finds that child labor is prevalent in the production of brick and garments, an industry that also is rife with forced labor.[13] Vietnam is the second-largest source of apparel and textile imports to the United States, estimated to total $7.9 billion in value; the industry employs more than 2 million workers.[14] Many of the clothes contain textiles produced in small workshops subcontracted to larger factories. These workshops

frequently use child labor, including forced labor involving the trafficking of children from rural areas into cities.[15]

While Vietnamese law bans forced labor and the mistreatment of workers, the government of Vietnam actively imposes compulsory labor on drug offenders. In these work centers, detainees are harassed and physically abused when they do not meet their daily factory quotas in so-called "labor therapy." An estimated 309,000 people were detained in Vietnam's drug detention centers from 2000 to 2010. The detainees receive little or no pay for their work.[16]

Brunei

The human rights situation in Brunei is dire. Last year, the sultan of Brunei, whose family has ruled Brunei for more than six centuries, imposed a strict penal code based on Sharia law. The Islamic criminal law includes punishments such as flogging, dismemberment and death by stoning for crimes such as adultery, alcohol consumption and homosexuality. Under emergency measures in place for 65 years, freedom of speech is severely limited,

and the country's legislature has a limited role.[17] Individuals have even been locked away for 10 years for wearing a Santa hat![18]

Many of the 85,000 migrant workers in Brunei also face labor exploitation and trafficking, related to debt bondage from labor recruitment fees, wage theft, passport confiscation, abuse and confinement. Domestic workers especially are prone to this kind of abuse. Immigration law allows for prison sentences and caning for workers who overstay their visas, fall into irregular status, or work or change employers without a permit.[19]

The government prohibits strikes, and the law makes no explicit provision for the right to collective bargaining. The law does not provide for reinstatement for dismissal related to union activity. There is only one active union in the country, the Brunei Oilfield Workers Union (BOWU), representing workers at Shell Petroleum. Government permission is required for holding a public meeting involving more than 10 people, and the police can break up any unofficial meeting of more than five people if they regard it as liable to disturb the peace.[20]

Conclusion

The U.S. government is seeking to grant increased trading privileges to countries with deeply troubling records of human and labor rights violations. There is little reason to believe the global community can push these countries to respect rights if they are to be rewarded with greater trading privileges without having to first undertake fundamental reforms. By not requiring fundamental changes first, the TPP gives away leverage. If workers do not have the legal freedoms to act collectively, they will not be able to exert the power needed to raise wages, increase worker protections or gain the social policies necessary for the creation of a middle class—something both labor and global corporations want. Without protection of core labor standards, including workers' right to organize unions and bargain collectively to improve wages and working conditions, global trade will continue a race to

the bottom in wages and working conditions, while its benefits will continue to go to a very small percentage of the elite and multinational corporations.

There currently is a lack of political will to enforce core labor standards and give workers bargaining power. A recent Government Accountability Office (GAO) report maintains that, in general, the USTR and the DOL have not systematically implemented all key elements of monitoring and enforcement with regard to FTA labor provisions.[21] This dynamic will not change with a labor chapter that does not make it mandatory to move labor cases quickly to their conclusion. If the TPP keeps the excessive discretion inherent in the current model, it will not improve the lives of TPP workers. The United States needs to reorient its trade policies. On labor, it must incorporate the ability to investigate and monitor labor rights abuses quickly and thoroughly. It must remove political obstacles to acting to protect what are recognized as fundamental human rights. Labor rights are essential to creating and growing an inclusive society with shared prosperity for all.

Successful trade policies must promote the fundamental labor rights included in the ILO core conventions; the preservation and expansion of public services; the creation of high-wage, high benefit jobs; the protection of democracy and allow public policies that regulate in the public interest. Global corporations are working to create a trading system which takes the power to regulate their behavior away from voters and national governments, and puts it at the international level, where there are no voters. This market fundamentalist approach does not and cannot work for workers. Successful trade policies must have at their core not simply "open markets" but improved lives for workers.

U.S. workers, and workers everywhere, need a 21st-century trade agreement that raises wages, enforces labor standards, creates decent work and helps ethical businesses export goods—not an agreement crafted to meet the whims of the largest corporations.

Endnotes

1 In a letter to the House of Representatives in October 2007, the AFL-CIO made clear that the May 2007 language was a first step: "We hope these new labor provisions will provide a starting point for future efforts to strengthen and effectively enforce protections for workers in the global economy. The new provisions will not solve all the problems workers face, but they will provide another important and useful tool to pressure governments and corporations to respect workers' fundamental human rights. But beyond the labor and environmental provisions of the Peru FTA, several issues of concern to working families, particularly with respect to investment, procurement and services, were not adequately addressed."

2 Ambassador Michael Froman, United States Trade Representative, "Written Statement: House Committee on Ways and Means," April 3, 2014. Available at http://waysandmeans.house.gov/uploadedfiles/att59846.pdf.

3 Other TPP countries also have a troubling record of labor rights violations that needs to be addressed; however, these four stand out in their severity.

4 "Law and Order in Mexico," The New York Times, Nov. 11, 2014. Available at www.nytimes.com/2014/11/12/opinion/murder-in-mexico.html?_r=0; "Mexico's Disappeared." Human Rights Watch, Feb. 20, 2013. Available at www.hrw.org/reports/2013/02/20/mexicos-disappeared-0.

5 Richard Marosi, "Product of Mexico," Los Angeles Times, Dec. 7, 2014. Available at http://graphics.latimes.com/product-of-mexico-camps/.

6 U.S. Department of Labor, ILAB, "List of Goods Produced by Child Labor or Forced Labor: Malaysia," 2014. Available at www.dol.gov/ilab/reports/child-labor/list-of-goods/countries/?q=Malaysia.

7 Office to Monitor and Combat Trafficking in Persons, 2014 Trafficking in Persons Report, "Malaysia." Available at www.state.gov/j/tip/rls/tiprpt/countries/2014/226770.htm.

8 Ibid.

9 Verité, "Forced Labor in the Production of Electronic Goods in Malaysia: A Comprehensive Study of Scope and Characteristics," 2014. Available at www.verite.org/research/electronicsmalaysia.

10 U.S. Department of State, "Vietnam 2013 Human Rights Report," 2013. Available at www.state.gov/documents/organization/220456.pdf.

11 ITUC, "Survey of violations of Trade Union Rights: Vietnam," 2014. Available at http://survey.ituc-csi.org/Vietnam.html?lang=en#tabs-3.

12 DOS, "Vietnam 2013 Human Rights Report." 2013.

13 DOL ILAB, "List of Goods Produced by Child Labor or Forced Labor: Vietnam," 2014. Available at www.dol.gov/ilab/reports/child-labor/list-of-goods/countries/?q=Vietnam.

14 Worker Rights Consortium, "Made in Vietnam," May 2013. Available at www.workersrights.org/linkeddocs/WRC_Vietnam_Briefing_Paper.pdf.

15 Ibid.

16 Adeline Zensius, "Forced Labor in Vietnam: A Violation of ILO Convention 29," International Labor Rights Forum, December 2011. Available at http://laborrightsblog.typepad.com/international_labor_right/2011/09/forced-labor-in-vietnam-a-violation-of-ilo-convention-29-.html#sthash.FJEFKvw8.dpuf.

17 DOS, "Brunei 2013 Human Rights Report," 2013. Available at www.state.gov/documents/organization/220391.pdf.

18 Richard Parry, "Brunei locks up Santa hat wearers for 5 years," Times UK, Jan. 10, 2015. Available at www.thetimes.co.uk/tto/news/world/asia/article4318997.ece.

19 DOS, "Brunei 2013 Human Rights Report," 2013.

20 ITUC, "2009 Annual Survey of violations of trade union rights—Brunei Darussalam," June 2009. Available at www.refworld.org/cgi-bin/texis/vtx/rwmain?page=country&category=&publisher=ITUC&type=&coi=BRN&rid=&docid=4c52cafdc&skip=0.

21 GAO, "Free Trade Agreements: U.S. Partners Are Addressing Labor Commitments, But More Monitoring and Enforcement Are Needed," 2014.

Mr. SALMON. Thank you, Ms. Drake.

I am going to start it off with a round of questions. My first question would be that the administration often mentions 21st century trade issues as a goal of TPP. What are these issues and why are they important to the U.S. economy?

Dr. Barfield, would you like to take a first crack at it?

Mr. BARFIELD. I think Scott went into this in some degree. There are issues that he talked about in terms of the new digital economy, of moving—and I should say that what has happened is that as the trade negotiations have gone over, over the decades, you have gone from trade barriers such as tariffs that were outside the border to the kinds of things that you find inside the border of regulations. And now we have new technologies such as the new digital economy which trade rules to date have not handled.

And so the term ''20th century agreement'' means that you are really looking at issues that have not been looked at before or only briefly looked at such as regulatory issues whether it is health and safety, whether it is environment or whatever. So it is in inside the border and regulatory framework that you are trying to change in the direction of allowing the free flow of trade and investment.

Mr. SALMON. Thank you.

Ms. Overby, did you, or Mr. Miller did you want——

Mr. MILLER. If I could add briefly. Yes, I agree with Claude. Classically defined as the electronic commerce and telecom issues, cross-border data flows being the most important for business operations, not just Internet firms and high tech firms but all firms operate with a lot of coordination. And free flow of data is critical to operation.

Second, in competition policy, which has been an older subject of trade, one of the things that is added in the TPP is the consideration of state-owned enterprises and how to treat state-owned enterprises and how to manage their competitive neutrality to make sure they operate the way that normal competitive companies do. I would also add regulatory cooperation or regulatory coherence is an important part. This is one of the behind the border issues that is a bigger part of trade frictions today than it was one or two decades ago.

Finally, in the intellectual property chapter, there is good work going on for safe harbors for Internet service providers which is consistent with U.S. law and practice, as well as measures to protect high technology innovators in foreign markets.

Mr. SALMON. One other question, Mr. Miller. Would those safeguards on these issues, whether for intellectual property or any of the other issues that you mentioned, would they happen if we are not part of it?

Mr. MILLER. It is unlikely. The United States has raised these issues. Frankly it is U.S. firms that are on the frontier of commercial innovation in these sectors. Mostly, in most trade negotiations economies raise the issues that are most important to their industries, and for the U.S. companies these come to a high level that probably wouldn't happen if we were absent from the TPP negotiations.

Mr. SALMON. One of the arguments against TPP is that our trade deficit with FTA partners has actually increased in aggregate.

However, my understanding is our overall trade deficit peaked in 2006 at $760 billion. Since then it has actually decreased to $505 billion. So trade balances with FTA partners have actually improved at least as far as I am reading the statistics. Is the trade deficit issue of particular concern to the negotiators? And should it be?

Ms. Overby, would you like to address that?

Ms. OVERBY. Thank you. Mr. Chairman, the trade balance is actually a poor measure of success of U.S. agreements. In macroeconomic terms, the U.S. overall trade deficit reflects an imbalance in our consumption and our savings, not our trade agreements. Until we save more than we consume, the U.S. will continue to run a deficit on a global basis. However, if we take as a group, the U.S. ran an aggregate trade surplus with its FTA partner countries in 2012 and 2013, and this surplus has grown since then. In fact, the U.S. has recorded a trade surplus in manufactured goods with its FTA partners for each of the past 5 years according to our Department of Commerce. This surplus reached $27 billion in 2009 and has expanded to $61 billion by 2013.

Mr. SALMON. Thank you.

I just have time for one more question. The issue of currency manipulation, is there any evidence that by itself currency manipulation is damaging to our economy?

Mr. MILLER. I am no expert on this matter, but I will take the advice of Fed Chairman Janet Yellen who was asked about currency manipulation and trade agreements at a recent Senate Banking Committee hearing. She mentioned, acknowledged the issue was an issue, but said that it was the United States had defensive issues here and that managing, doing her job of managing U.S. fiscal policy might be constrained if we were to negotiate this in trade agreements.

I would note also there are certain things that are important to trade and affect trade that we don't consider in trade agreements. I would note farm subsidies is one of those. I don't think there is any debate that farm subsidies do have an effect on farm pricing, but the United States has never negotiated them within a bilateral free trade agreement.

Mr. SALMON. Ms. Overby?

Ms. OVERBY. Yes. On currency we agree. Currency manipulation is a very serious problem in international trade, and we are encouraged that the administration and Congress are working to find solutions. The Chamber's view is that disputes over currency deserve a full airing, but the questions are what is the right forum, and what measures can be effective? Historically, governments have tackled currency matters in a very broad fora such as the IMF, G20 or G7. This is because governments have seen currency valuation and current account imbalances as global in nature and not effectively addressed with a single partner or a small collection of partners.

Most international policymakers and experts want to be sure that we don't tie the hands of the Fed or the Treasury Department with enforceable currency provisions in TPP or any U.S. trade agreement. Our institutions need to be able to determine our own monetary and fiscal policies and be able to respond in a crisis. The other TPP partners have as Mr. Sherman mentioned indicated that they do not want currency provisions in an agreement.

Mr. SALMON. Thank you, I have run out of time.

Mr. Sherman?

Mr. SHERMAN. Just for the record, using ITC data, our trade relationship with our FTA partners most recent statistics, $180 billion deficit in merchandise plus 70—see, I can add and subtract—billion in services. That is $110 billion trade deficit with the FTA countries.

I do serve on the House Financial Services Committee, and have for 18 years. There is a huge difference between setting your interest rates for your own national economic growth on the one hand, and intervening in currency markets to push down your currency and steal jobs on the other. And only when those two are conflated could somebody say, oh, we better not talk about currency manipulation, somebody will try to tie the hands of the Fed.

And I would point out that the statistics I gave you don't even count the re-exports, situations where goods are brought into the United States for transit often to a Latin American country. We are told that this agreement is going to help us vis-à-vis our national security relationship with China, but we are also told China might join the agreement. You can't argue it both ways.

But when it comes to national security in China and the idea of binding us to other Asian nations let us look at the situation. We are already devoting all of our procurement and research dollars at the Pentagon to figure out how to fight China for the benefit of Japan, Korea, et cetera, over some relatively useless Pacific islets, rocks. And so we are going to spend and perhaps die for their territory and now we have to give them a lot of jobs to get them to let us do it. That is, if being their security is not enough and we have to give up jobs, I would be surprised.

First, I want to thank the first three witnesses for not asserting that this agreement under consideration would lead to more jobs or would reduce the trade deficit, because it obviously won't. Ms. Overby has made the point that workers are discouraged and they are not entering the workforce. The reason for that is for low wages, and the reason for that is the trade policy that we have suffered.

For every job we lose in these trade agreements there are ten others where people don't get raises because their employer is able to say I may move to China or I have to compete with China, or I have to compete with the free trade agreement from Korea, et cetera, and so wages are low and you end up with low participation rates.

As to national security, national security is not just figuring out how to fight over rocks on the Pacific. It is also Iran. And there is one thing that Obama and Netanyahu agree on, and that is the key thing here is sanctions, they just disagree on how to modulate them in order to get what they hope is a good deal. Under these fair trade agreements, those provisions of our sanctions aimed at U.S. contractors could be swept away.

Dr. Barfield, is there anything in the agreement that you are aware of that will say that those U.S. sanctions, particularly government procurement sanctions, will be fully enforced notwithstanding the FTA?

Mr. BARFIELD. Well, the government procurement is one of the things being negotiated in the TPP.

Mr. SHERMAN. Okay. All of our past free trade agreements open giant loopholes in the number one national security effort of this country and that is imposing sanctions on Iran until we get a good deal.

Ms. Drake, what is it like to be a labor organizer in Vietnam? And I realize just because you work for the AFL–CIO doesn't mean you are in the organizing department. But you might know some of those folks.

Ms. DRAKE. Good question. I mean the real thing that you are risking that you are not necessarily risking here in the United States is you can be arrested. And when you are arrested there are issues of extrajudicial killings and beatings by the police in Vietnam. But, really, you just don't have the opportunity to say we want our own union, we want an independent union, we want to get together and work with each other for better. There is one national federation, the VGCL, and it is really an arm of the government. And while it does function, it doesn't function as a union. It sort of makes sure that you get birthday cake at work when it is your birthday and things of this nature. It doesn't really function as a tool to say workers here need more safety, they need more money, they need better benefits. These are the things that workers need.

Mr. SHERMAN. A number of the witnesses gave us a tremendous picture of how Asia is big, important, dynamic, and growing in every respect. Couldn't agree with you more. That is why we needed to use the threat of dramatically increased tariffs, and even with the WTO we can, whether we choose to our not, just impose them or threaten to impose them in order to secure free trade agreements. And so I look forward to us having the right trade policy toward this important and dynamic region.

And finally, we have a huge trade deficit. We used to blame the U.S. Federal deficit. Well, we ran a surplus under Clinton, we had a huge trade deficit. We had deficits at the Federal level. We have a huge trade deficit. On rainy days we have a trade deficit. On sunny days we have a trade deficit.

And so ultimately we are told it is because your workers aren't producing products at a good price that the world wants to buy. And I would say we have the best workers in the world. We have the best scientists in the world. We have the best entrepreneurs in the world. But we have the largest trade deficit in the world because we have the worst trade policy in the world.

I yield back.

Mr. BARFIELD. I would like to challenge that if I could.

Mr. SHERMAN. I believe my time has expired.

Mr. BARFIELD. All right, I will do it on somebody else's.

Mr. SALMON. Mr. Emmer?

Mr. EMMER. Why don't you go ahead, Mr. Barfield, and then thank you, Mr. Chair.

Mr. BARFIELD. Well, the point is that nobody has said that the trade deficit causes jobs or that the trade, not here at any rate. I don't know what the AFL–CIO, what my colleague there would say. But to keep coming back to something that this trade agreement ignored was Tami's point that we have to keep coming back to. It's economics 101 that we will run the trade deficit with the rest of the world overall as long as we do not save, invest and save enough both privately and publicly to cover our investments and what we are spending. And the United States has for the last several decades not been able to do that.

So you can change the trade deficit with China or shift it toward Japan or whatever way you want to do but overall, as Tami pointed out, it is the macroeconomic factors. You are still going to have a large trade deficit unless you change that. And we have been unwilling to do that. This is not to let China fall free.

Mr. EMMER. Mr. Barfield, if you don't mind, and I appreciate it. Maybe you can filter it in to some of the others. I have just a couple minutes left, and I thank the chair for letting me ask a couple of questions.

I am from the state of Minnesota, and in 2013 Minnesota goods exported were 20.8 billion. Nationally, and this is not just Minnesota, jobs supported by exports reached more than 11 million in 2013, and every billion dollars of United States exports of goods supported an estimated 5,400 jobs in that same year. By the way, jobs supported by exports, goods that were exported, paid an estimated 13 to 18 percent above the national average. It is important to my state because 47 percent of Minnesota's exports, again in that year, almost $10 billion went to countries that are currently part of this negotiation.

Mr. Barfield, very quickly I want to cover a couple of areas if I have time. First, I hear a lot of people, and I see some T-shirts here about Fast Track authority. Under the Constitution it is my understanding, Article I Section 8, that Congress has the sole authority to enter into agreements with foreign nations whether they be treaties or trade agreements, and that the executive has only authority to negotiate. Is my understanding correct?

Mr. BARFIELD. Yes.

Mr. EMMER. Now the idea that this is going to be sight unseen—and I am going to move to Ms. Overby. There was a statement made, I think by Ms. Drake, that Congress if it passes trade promotion authority which is nothing more than legislation that tells the executive branch this is what the expectations are; this is what we can do, what we can't do; this is what we will accept, what we won't; this is what Congress is doing to exercise its constitutional authority over trade; the testimony was made that this will somehow come to Congress sight unseen.

In fact, the TPP legislation that would be part of this if this is going to go forward would require that you have full transparency. Isn't that right, Ms. Overby? And could you please explain what that would mean.

Ms. OVERBY. Thank you. Yes, you are absolutely correct. I also find it somewhat ironic that critics of the TPP negotiations and specific chapters or provisions always criticize the lack of transparency in the negotiations, but in the very next breath they say it is about agreement. If it is not transparent, I am not sure how one knows whether it is good or bad.

Also calls to make confidential negotiating text public are, in my view, misguided. Disclosure of negotiating text would risk giving foreign governments a road map to U.S. sensitivities and red lines that could be used to our disadvantage. I was actually in Korea working for the American Chamber of Commerce in Korea when the U.S. and Korea were negotiating the KORUS FTA. And an opponent of the KORUS FTA from the Korean National Assembly leaked some text, and I saw it firsthand that it provided our negotiators a clear picture of their strategy and frankly it helped us. We got a better deal, from our perspective, because of that.

Mr. EMMER. Quickly, can you address the other claim that this is somehow going to affect jobs in this country? Because my understanding is the tariffs, in other words the barriers to products coming into our country are among the lowest in the world. And actually we want to make sure that our labor, our greatest workers on the face of the planet, are able to produce and sell their products fairly in markets outside of our country.

Ms. OVERBY. You are exactly right. The U.S. already has one of the lowest tariffs in the world and most of Asia has very high. In fact, in Southeast Asia five times the tariff level to Americans. So our market is already open. If we do nothing, what that means is they keep selling to the U.S. and we can't sell to them.

Mr. EMMER. Wouldn't that affect the trade deficit?

Ms. OVERBY. In a very negative way, exactly. And your point about jobs, you are absolutely right. It will have an impact. This agreement is a job creating agreement because it is going to allow us to sell more, and when we sell more we have to hire more people to do it. Thank you.

Mr. EMMER. Thank you very much. Thank you, Mr. Chair.

Mr. SALMON. Thank you.

Ms. Gabbard?

Ms. GABBARD. Thank you very much, Mr. Chairman. Obviously this entire discussion is very important, and you mentioned looking at this. This is macroeconomics. There have been a lack of details that members have been able to share with people at home who have not a background in economics but who are very interested specifically in how this will affect me and my family, our ability to support them, and to be able to have opportunity to create jobs.

I want to touch on the compliance issue because I think it is a valid one. When we are talking about whether it is labor standards or environmental standards or other things that the administration has put out there saying, hey, don't worry, we are going to ensure that these standards are included—really, there is not a great track record in history of such standards having been enforced either recently or in previous history.

So I would like to ask you what gives you such great confidence that these standards if met in the agreement would be enforced and what is the enforcement mechanism?

Mr. MILLER. Well, I would just note that with regard to labor and environmental standards we have actually come a very long way since the NAFTA. In the NAFTA in 1994, the labor and environmental provisions were so-called side agreements. They were not in the body of the text. They were basically voluntary cooperation agreements.

Since that time there have been a number of iterations in U.S. policy. We moved to a standard in 2001–2002 so-called the ''enforce your own laws.'' Thanks to the leadership of at that time Chairman Levin and others, in the May 10th, 2007 agreement there was a higher standard promulgated which first tied the standards for labor and environment to international obligations; and second, allowed the same kind of dispute settlement mechanism as for any other violation of the free trade agreement.

So the way our current law and our current negotiating policy operates is that the labor and environment chapter have equal standing with every other chapter in the trade agreement in terms of access to dispute settlement. There is a current live dispute settlement for the labor provision of the Central America Free Trade Agreement which is happening in real time right now so that would be the easiest one to follow.

But I would note importantly on the environmental side, an important advance is if any two parties to, say, the TPP are parties to a separate environmental accord, like the CITES agreement or some other environmental accord, and there is an alleged violation of that separate accord that those parties can use the TPP dispute settlement chapter to settle the dispute of an outside agreement. So I think we made progress. Thank you.

Ms. GABBARD. Thank you.

Ms. Drake?

Ms. DRAKE. Thank you very much. I think in terms of compliance it is a particularly important question. We have under CAFTA a complaint against Guatemala. There is actually several live complaints. The one against Guatemala has been going on for 6 years, and that means for 6 years employers in Guatemala have been freely driving down wages by failing to pay minimum wage, by firing workers who try to form a union, by specifically not following the law.

And while they are driving down wages in Guatemala that means they are also driving down wages in nearby Honduras and El Salvador and Costa Rica because it is one labor market. And by the way they are also driving down wages here because employers here say if you don't take pay cuts, if you don't give back seniority rights, if you don't give up your pension plan we are going to move production to Central America. So it is a critical issue.

On the Honduras issue, which is also an open complaint, that one was open for 3 years even before the administration responded. And they just put out a report last Friday. It is a great report. They may do some things to improve labor rights in Honduras, but meanwhile workers on the ground are being abused every single day. And that sends the wrong message to our TPP partners about how seriously the labor commitments will be taken.

But also if the chapter doesn't include specific timelines, requirements to act on complaints that have merit, then the problem is, is that any government that doesn't want to act, if it has unlimited discretion, can just ignore it. They can do far worse than delay for 3 years. This is an administration that cares about labor rights. What if we have an administration, President X, in 2017 who doesn't care at all about labor rights?

Ms. GABBARD. Thank you.

Thank you, Mr. Chairman.

Mr. SALMON. Mr. Connolly?

Mr. CONNOLLY. Thank you, Mr. Chairman.

I thank you all for being here today. I must confess part of my problem with this topic is we now have taken theological positions. So largely, the AFL, almost no free trade agreement could ever be good. They are all bad. They all create dislocations. They kill jobs. They haven't worked out. And there is no reason to be confident that any enforcement mechanism would ever really work.

Similarly, the Chamber of Commerce hasn't found one it doesn't like. And Ms. Overby you have heard me give this sermon before, but Ms. Drake's last point, what confidence does somebody on my side of the aisle have that the Chamber would ever really seriously care about labor suppression overseas when the Chamber is actively engaged in funneling money to campaigns for labor suppression here at home?

And so is someone like me who is inclined intellectually to be open to free trade, I couldn't possibly trust the Chamber, politically or substantively, to take that issue Ms. Drake has just given us as seriously. You have given, not you personally, Ms. Overby, but the Chamber, I mean if you have a D after your name then the Chamber is going to go after you. It might pick one or two, and I mean one or two token Democrats, and other than that it doesn't matter what our free trade record is. There is no reward whatsoever coming out of your organization and Mr. Donohue, and so we vote for free trade at our peril.

And I think framing this issue theologically and the political sort of brittleness that attends to that does not contribute to a rational debate or discussion about the real merits and real problems associated with any free trade agreement.

Mr. Miller, I take your point. I mean if you listen to the critics of NAFTA it is a complete failure and it didn't address these issues, and if that critique conceded, if that is true, then why would anybody have confidence in the argument, well, this time we got it right, trust us.

Mr. BARFIELD. I would like to turn that around if I could.

Mr. CONNOLLY. Okay, go ahead, Dr. Barfield.

Mr. BARFIELD. Sorry. I would turn that around and give the example that I did just in terms of geostrategic, but I would also do it in terms of the economics. Why was it that President Obama turned around? Why does he think—this is a very progressive, a very liberal administration. And the President came into office saying that he would not have voted for NAFTA and he didn't like the free trade agreements that the Bush administration. The TPP is building on that tradition which causes the AF of L–CIO a good deal of heartburn, but the President has turned around because he thinks that it is possible.

Mr. CONNOLLY. Well, Dr. Barfield——

Mr. BARFIELD. And it is not the Chamber we are talking about here. This is the leader of your party.

Mr. CONNOLLY. Well, he is also the leader of the country. He is your President as well as mine.

Mr. BARFIELD. I was not implying he wasn't.

Mr. CONNOLLY. I understand.

Mr. BARFIELD. I have defended——

Mr. CONNOLLY. I just thought I would say that. But I would also point out to you that is not unique to this President. Name a President, Democrat or Republican, who hasn't come around to the idea that free trade makes sense and hasn't gotten behind free trade on——

Mr. BARFIELD. Why do you think that is the case? It is not——

Mr. CONNOLLY. Ms. Drake may have a point of view about that. Do you want to answer that?

Ms. DRAKE. I would like to answer that. I think that candidates in general, writ large, are saying what voters want to hear when they are running. And they get it. They hear people. They say my wages have been stagnant. They say my uncle was laid off from a good factory job. They go to main streets and they see what is happening when a factory closes and a town dies out. And then you get into a position of power and the choices that you make are different, and the influences on you are different. So it is disappointing when candidate after candidate runs in a particular way and then votes differently.

But I would like to get to your question of, the AFL–CIO is ideological on this and I don't think——

Mr. CONNOLLY. And so is the Chamber.

Ms. DRAKE. Well, look, we——

Mr. CONNOLLY. And if you are going to answer that Ms. Overby has to have the opportunity too.

Ms. DRAKE. We submitted 34 pages in January 2010 of this is what the TPP should like if we are going to support it, which by the way I also want to challenge Ms. Overby's comment that we are always saying it is a bad deal. What I said was the questions about the TPP are far too complex to merit a grant of Fast Track.

The AFL–CIO has not taken a position for or against the TPP. We are certainly against using NAFTA as a model, using Korea as a model, using failed models as a model. And from what has been said publicly about the TPP, which is frankly very little in comparison to the voluminous number of pages, it is using NAFTA and Korea as a model.

Mr. CONNOLLY. Okay, thank you. And by the way the word was ''theological'' not ''ideological.'' My background, I hear theology.

If the chairman would just allow the Chamber rep to respond similarly and then I am done.

Mr. SALMON. Yes, that is fine.

Mr. CONNOLLY. I thank the chair.

Ms. OVERBY. It is always a pleasure to see, as a constituent in Mr. Connolly's district it is always a pleasure to see my member. So how are you?

Mr. CONNOLLY. Yes, every day is a holiday around here.

Ms. OVERBY. Isn't it? I just want to make a couple of very brief comments. You know where the Chamber stands. You know how the Chamber determines their political donations. I am not the person to address that. But I do want to talk about failed agreements and why so little has been written about TPP.

Again the reality is the negotiation is ongoing and frankly a lot of what has been written from America is not helping America's negotiators. And if we all want the best deal America can get I would think we would be standing behind the United States.

To my colleague on the right, Dr. Barfield, why did President Obama change his view? Well, we worked very closely with the administration on KORUS, on the Korea FTA, and I believe he changed his view because he felt he got a deal he could sell. A deal that improved the auto piece, and he was able to get not only Ford Motor Company, but if I am not wrong the UAW actually supported KORUS.

But I will make, and certainly admit that no trade agreement is perfect. We continue to try to improve upon it. I will say that the KORUS agreement is better than earlier agreements particularly in the area of enforcement. Nineteen committees were set up under KORUS and each one of those committees has a senior government-to-government working level meeting where we are able to raise our issues much faster. I believe the TPP will have even better enforcement mechanisms. I think our USTR representative is well aware that other countries are not always playing with the same level playing field and so they are giving us our opportunity to try to improve it faster.

Mr. CONNOLLY. I think I am going to have to cut that off, otherwise Ms. Drake is—I will say my point about the Chamber was much broader than who you contribute to. It was a pattern of exclusion that I think impinges on our ability up here to have a reward and punishment system that is a little more rational than it otherwise is on this subject. Thank you.

Mr. SALMON. Thank you.

Mr. Grayson?

Mr. GRAYSON. Thank you.

Ms. Drake, will the Trans-Pacific Partnership decrease or increase America's trade deficit?

Ms. DRAKE. It is impossible to know because it is mostly secret, but it seems likely poised to increase the U.S. trade deficit.

Mr. GRAYSON. What makes you say that?

Ms. DRAKE. Well, for one thing it doesn't deal, according to the President, with currency. And as Mr. Barfield was explaining before with trade deficits, what he didn't mention was that basic trade 101 theory says if a country is running trade deficits over time, currencies will fluctuate to account for that and it will eventually even out. The United States is the only country that we know of in the history of the world that has had such large and sustained trade deficits over time.

And while it is true that the United States has very low tariffs and very low trade barriers, the reason that we think we have seen floods of imports back in from certain trade agreements is not because the firms, the domestic firms in those countries are now exporting more than they could, it is often that production that used to happen in the U.S. has moved to a trading partner country and then that offshore production is taking advantage of the lower tariffs to get those goods back into the U.S.

Mr. GRAYSON. Ms. Overby, will the Trans-Pacific Partnership decrease or increase the U.S. trade deficit?

Ms. OVERBY. I believe it will decrease it because the studies seem to show that with our FTA trading partners we tend to have surpluses.

Mr. GRAYSON. Well, but isn't it true, Ms. Overby, that since NAFTA went into effect, the first of these major trade agreements, the United States has run a trade deficit of at least $135 billion every single year, and therefore doesn't it follow that if we continue to expand these trade agreements we will have higher and higher not lower and lower trade deficits?

Mr. BARFIELD. No.

Mr. GRAYSON. No, no. I am still with Ms. Overby there.

Ms. OVERBY. I am not an expert in the NAFTA numbers, but everything I have heard and been told, no, those numbers are inaccurate.

Mr. GRAYSON. You are saying that the numbers I just gave you are inaccurate?

Ms. OVERBY. May I——

Mr. GRAYSON. The fact that since NAFTA went into effect, every single year we have had a trade deficit of $135 billion or more, you are saying that is inaccurate?

Mr. BARFIELD. I don't——

Mr. GRAYSON. No, sorry. Still with Ms. Overby. Sorry. Let us stick with the witness here.

Ms. OVERBY. I am sorry, I don't have that information.

Mr. GRAYSON. Okay. Now here is another little tidbit for you. In the last 14 years we have run the largest trade deficits in the history of the planet. And in the last 14 years we have followed these trade agreements and had an open trade policy. What makes you think that that would reverse itself under the Trans-Pacific Partnership?

Ms. OVERBY. Okay, may I answer?

Mr. GRAYSON. I am asking you to answer.

Ms. OVERBY. I would love to. Again in macroeconomic terms, the trade deficit reflects the imbalance in consumption and savings. It is not our trade agreements. If you want America to have a trade surplus, may I suggest that Congress pass a budget that is saving more than we spend.

Mr. GRAYSON. Listen, I am talking to you about the trade deficit not the Federal deficit, so don't change the subject. But let us continue it in this vein if we can.

Since we adopted the trade policy starting with NAFTA and entered into these free trade agreements, our cumulative trade deficit is $11 trillion. That is over $35,000 for every single man, woman and child in this country. For me and my five children that is about $200,000. What makes you think that the Trans-Pacific Partnership, which is something like the tenth or eleventh in a long series of these trade giveaways, is somehow magically going to reverse that pattern?

Ms. OVERBY. I don't think I can give you an answer that is going to change your mind.

Mr. GRAYSON. Why don't you give me an answer that is accurate?

Ms. OVERBY. Okay. Again I believe that the overall trade deficit has nothing to do with the trade agreement. I think it is about the imbalance in our consumption and savings.

Mr. GRAYSON. Okay, so you do think it is just this magnificent coincidence that since we adopted these policies we have had these enormous, staggering trade deficits year after year?

Ms. OVERBY. No, I think it is the way we spend more than, we consume more than we save. And also the U.S. dollar is the currency around the world. I mean we are the reserve currency.

Mr. GRAYSON. We were the reserve currency for the past 100 years, and it is only since NAFTA went into effect that this happened.

What about you, Mr. Miller? What do you have to say about this subject?

Mr. MILLER. Well, I would observe that the United States trade deficit fell by 46 percent in 2009 versus 2008.

Mr. GRAYSON. That has something to do with the fact that we had a worldwide depression in 2008.

Mr. MILLER. It certainly did. It had everything to do with it.

Mr. GRAYSON. Okay, but you are not playing fair.

Mr. MILLER. If I could finish.

Mr. GRAYSON. You are coming up with a factoid that has nothing to do with my question.

Mr. MILLER. My point is there was no change in trade policy year on year.

Mr. GRAYSON. No, just a collapse of the world economy and——

Mr. MILLER. Yes, so that is—I am suggesting there are other factors involved in the overall trade deficit.

Mr. GRAYSON. All right, my time is up. Thank you.

Mr. SALMON. Now that the committee members both majority and minority have had an opportunity to question the witnesses, I ask unanimous consent to recognize Representative Marcy Kaptur. Hearing no objections, I recognize Representative Kaptur.

Ms. KAPTUR. Chairman Salmon, thank you very much for the opportunity to be here today. And I guess I am just sitting here looking at what is going on in the world and being very thankful that we are citizens of this republic, and whether we agree or disagree we are going to work this out. It is going to take us time because it really isn't working for America right now, our trade policy, but when we look at other places I am just thankful that we live in the system that we do.

Let me say that for those representing the business community, Dr. Barfield, Ms. Overby and Mr. Miller, I respect what you do and you have to be part of the solution to help us fix what is wrong with our trade policy. We can't do it without you as a country. I am in the freedom business, and so it is a different business than those you represent are in.

Ms. Drake, thank you for being here on behalf of many workers who live in the district that I represent and understanding the travails that they have experienced as a result of these trade agreements. Many times having to pack up boxes with the machines in the companies in which they worked and going to a foreign country to train their replacements. Can you imagine how horrible that experience is? And so I appreciate the moment to give a little reflection here.

Dr. Barfield, I agree with you that our trade policy has been used for advancing national strategic interests. Oh, do I agree with that statement. And the problem with that is that it currently, our trade deficits now cut about a fifth, maybe a little bit less than that, about 16.5 percent, 16.7 percent off our GDP annually.

And unfortunately trade in the aggregate is not helping us domestically. In places like I represent, the average worker has lost $7,000 a year in wages, and what families are facing is extraordinarily difficult. And what is dangerous for liberty is these people aren't voting. They are not voting for Republicans. They are not voting for Democrats. They are stopping their belief that this country can work for them.

So in our conversation today, I wanted to place on the record since 1975 the country has accumulated $9.5 trillion in trade deficit. Congressman Grayson used an $11 trillion figure, so depending on which year you start with that is pretty significant. It has never happened in this country before. That translates, using 5,000 jobs per billion, into a loss of 47,500,000 jobs. Some of the workers who haven't been able to find work live in the district that I represent.

When you have something that cuts nearly a fifth of your GDP and loses that many jobs, we have a budget deficit because we have a trade deficit. And for what Ms. Overby said about savings, if you are an individual why would you put any money in a bank today? You can't even earn 1 percent interest on it. So there is no incentive for savings anymore because we have doled out almost a fifth of our ability to produce.

So on Mexico let me just say I was here when NAFTA first passed. They said we would have trade balance. We have had trade deficits every year from Mexico. This past year 2014 there was a $99 billion, a nearly $100 billion trade deficit with Mexico. That has been the same over the last 3 years hovering around $100 billion.

For Korea, last year it was 26 billion. We were supposed to have more exports to Korea. We were supposed to get 50,000 cars into Korea while they sent 500,000 here. We never got to 50,000. I don't even know if we are up to 5,000 yet. We may be at 500. My point is that the numbers aren't working for us. If we had done it right under George Bush the first and Bill Clinton, to be a freedom lover we should have had a major Trans-Atlantic free trade agreements with countries that abide by rule of law. We didn't do that. We didn't do that. We signed agreements with places that have closed markets; that don't believe in liberty; and I can't tell you how many companies I represent that have had trouble in their dealings in China. There is no rule of law.

So I am just saying to you, as patriotic Americans we have got to fix this. We have got to first support liberty and we have got to create economic agreements that work for our people, and that isn't happening. And the tragedy in the street with these people who think about national strategic interests and so forth, they forget about what happens within our own borders. The people at the National Security Council, they know every other country in the world. They sort of forget about us and what happens to the people that we represent.

So I wanted to place that statement on the record. I hope that this won't be the last hearing that this committee holds. I can't believe in TPP because I have been here long enough to see what happened with NAFTA, what happened with Korea. The Jordan accord I voted for and that one we are still in balance. That had labor provisions. It had environmental. That might be a better measure, a better type of agreement, but we basically failed as a country when we did not uphold the rule of law.

Many of you are lawyers, and when we got into agreements with countries that don't abide by the rule of law we really got in a cul-de-sac and we are in it until today. So I put that on the record. I hope you all have ideas about how to restore trade balance to this country, because we can't continue to hemorrhage this way. It is hurting our republic deeply. It is hurting it, not, ma'am, only macroeconomically, but microeconomically. On the street. The places that each of us represents a piece of the puzzle.

So I appreciate the graciousness of this committee for allowing me to place that statement on the record. If anybody wants to respond and there is still time, certainly they can. Thank you.

Mr. BARFIELD. Well, I guess I am heartened to know that it sounds as if you will support the U.S.-European Free Trade Agreement when it comes to force over the next year.

But I would like to go back to the point, I know we have been over this again and again, but I think on my side I do not represent the business community. I am a think tank. Sometimes they don't like what we say. Sometimes they do, sometimes they don't.

I would like to—I know we have said it, but coming back to whether it was NAFTA or other agreements where Jordan was in balance that it somehow that had to do with the standard of living in the United States that is simply not true. As we have said, where the United States has to look in terms of our trade deficit is not with trade agreements but our own internal policies.

And the other odd thing that I will throw in as a ringer here right at the end is that trade deficits are not necessarily evidence of noncompetitiveness nor of killing jobs. We were in, in the 1990s which is supposedly a golden period under Bill Clinton, increasing trade deficits where we had increasing job creation in the United States.

Trade deficit, you have to find the circumstances. The reason we did, which is another reason we will probably have an increased trade deficit over the next couple of years if things go well for us, is that the United States was outgrowing, outperforming other nations. We were consuming more and we were creating more jobs. And so the trade deficit did not in that case translate into some lack of competitiveness. It is likely not to do the same thing in the next couple of years if the United States keeps on the same——

Ms. KAPTUR. I would love to invite you all to the district that I represent and we can talk trade on the street.

Mr. BARFIELD. Happy to do that.

Ms. KAPTUR. And it would be very enlightening. Very, very enlightening. So——

Mr. SALMON. Sounds like it might make for a good Town Hall.

Ms. KAPTUR. How about that?

Mr. SALMON. There you go.

Ms. Overby?

Ms. KAPTUR. Meet the street. Mr. Chairman, if I could just say, because you have been so generous to me, I just want to say that in terms of the Transatlantic Alliance, if we had formed it, those nations that are unfree by any measure could have been invited to join in and we would have raised the potential for liberty globally. We haven't done that.

Look at what has happened to Mexico. Just look what has happened there. And we didn't address closed markets. Go to Japan, less than 3 percent of the cars on their street today are from anyplace else in the world but Japan. And we have the most open market in the world. You can't have free trade agreements when you have closed markets and when you have state-run capitalism like is happening in China.

We are really living in a false world in some ways. We are not looking at the values of liberty and rule of law in these agreements and it is hurting us greatly. And it is hurting liberty. It is hurting liberty globally. So I thank you, Mr. Chairman, very much.

Mr. SALMON. Thank you.

Ms. Overby, it is back to my time but I am going to let you answer.

Ms. OVERBY. Two brief comments on Japan and it being a closed market, and the numbers on cars. I do think that TPP provides us the best opportunity that we are going to see in our lifetime to try to crack open that market. And referring to job loss, I think everyone here really needs to take a look at the fact that—one of my colleagues loves to say, yes, jobs have been lost to that country called productivity. Technological innovations. The market, the world has changed. The number of people needed to make products is shrinking dramatically. That is not trade's fault. That is the technology growth that we are, we live in a technological age. Thank you.

Mr. SALMON. So I have a couple of questions to ask. But before I do, the absolutism that Representative Grayson mentioned a few minutes ago, that all these terrible things with our trade deficit have coincided with the trade agreements, it is like saying—we created the Federal Department of Education in 1979. At the time in the 1970s we were at the top of the charts in every field and now we are 14th in math and sciences in the world. Does that mean that the creation of the Department of Education actually made us do worse in education? I don't think that anybody is necessarily going to make that argument. I think that there are a whole host of issues that impact our trade deficit and that is what we are talking about. You talked about a few of the issues.

But I want to ask another question. If we don't participate in TPP, if the United States does not agree to participate in TPP and China goes ahead with its plans with RCEP and their free trade agreement, is there anything that stops American companies from exporting jobs overseas or outsourcing then, even if we don't participate? Anybody care to respond to that?

Mr. MILLER. There are important consequences to not concluding the Trans-Pacific Partnership. We would walk away from potential market access gains in economies that we do not now have FTAs with. There are five of them. There would be an immediate loss in reputation. My belief is the Obama administration has staked a great deal of prestige on the completion of the Trans-Pacific Partnership, and our Asian allies and friends and partners would look differently at us.

In the long run, my view is that the world economy will continue to grow and——

Mr. SALMON. As it always has.

Mr. MILLER. As it always has. And the world won't wait for us. And that I think American firms and workers are best served when America leads in writing the rules. That has been true since the Bretton Woods Conference. The U.S. has been the defender of an open rules-based trading system. It is vitally important. And for me, that is what TPP and TTIP with Europeans is a real continuation of.

Mr. SALMON. So as far as my question though, I mean if we didn't do TPP does that mean that jobs won't still continue to go overseas?

Mr. MILLER. Well, you will still have globalization.

Mr. SALMON. That is my point.

Mr. MILLER. It will be easier. With TPP it makes it easier for us to compete, I think.

Mr. SALMON. Right.

Mr. MILLER. Because as we have said several times here, we have lower tariffs, we have more open borders than others with certain exceptions we want to be clear about, in sugar and things like that but we are the ones who are more open. So it is the rest of world, not entirely but to some degree.

I would like though come back to a point I made at the beginning in terms of what would happen if we don't do the TPP. I keep coming back to the fact that the geostrategic and the geoeconomic are linked. The United States in the next few years, whoever the new President is or whatever the new, whichever party has the Congress, has a good deal of heavy responsibilities around the world that are security responsibilities. There are those who argue that now we are not really committing enough resources to live up to the so-called pivot or balance. Scholars at my institute believe that.

But wherever one stands on that question it is certainly true that the United States has got a lot of difficult questions to work through in terms of where it is going to put its resources both domestic and in terms of national security over the next few years. I think this is where the trade agreements does link in. I think it will be a lot easier to persuade the Congress and the American people to support a leadership role in Asia if we are a part of a regional economic structure that is thriving and is successful for U.S. businesses and U.S. workers. And that is where they are tied together.

Mr. SALMON. And finally, Ms. Kaptur made some very impassioned points and I appreciate them. As far as liberty and freedom and the principles that we stand for maybe Ronald Reagan said it best, the shining city on a hill. If we are not at the table, how are they impacted by the things that we believe?

I think that the most important thing that we export is not a commodity, it is actually an ideal. And that ideal is freedom. It is the thing that we stand for. And I don't know any relationship that I have ever had with anybody—my wife, my children, friends, enemies—that I have ever improved one iota by not being at the table, by not engaging, by not being there communicating and actively working with them.

Heaven help us if what we stand for and what we believe is not a part of the equation and if RCEP which China is pushing ends up being the free trade agreement for the region instead of what we are pushing. I far more trust the values that we advocate and the things that we stand for rather than what China stands for.

Anyway go ahead, Ms. Overby.

Ms. OVERBY. Yes, Mr. Chairman, I just wanted to make the comment that what happens if TPP fails? Well, then the small and medium sized companies in America lose. Many opponents always talk about the large multinational American companies and they will be okay one way or another. But the SMEs——

Mr. SALMON. They always seem to be.

Ms. OVERBY. They seem to survive. But the small and medium sized companies they will be grossly disadvantaged. Because as we all know our market is open. All TPP is going to do is to try to knock down some of the barriers on the other side. Tariffs are a big part of it but it is more than tariffs. The problems these days are behind the border. Countries have gotten very creative in throwing up new non-tariff barriers, whether it is standards or rules it makes it so hard for American companies to compete.

So all we are asking for is simply our Government to help us try to knock down those barriers, and if we do nothing America loses because the rest of the world is not going to stand by. I am in Asia most of the year and China is everywhere. They are very aggressive. They are pushing RCEP. They are doing all kinds of soft diplomacy. And America will lose if we do nothing.

Mr. SALMON. Thank you.

Mr. Sherman?

Mr. SHERMAN. We are told that we need to be proud of these trade rules because they were made in America. These are trade rules made in America that make sure that nothing else will be made in America. We should be as proud of these trade rules as the Spaniards are of the Spanish flu, both have wrecked incredible destruction.

We are told that the President's credibility and prestige is on the line. No, his credibility and prestige is on the line with Obamacare. And those who want to say that should be advocating every day for whatever technical fixes are necessary to make sure that Obamacare goes on and subsidies are provided regardless of how the Supreme Court interprets the current draft.

We are told that the only choice is between the failure we currently have and the failure that is being proposed. No one here with the exception of Ms. Drake even acknowledges the fact that I proposed a different trade approach. That is to say to threaten to raise dramatically our tariffs with or without compliance in WTO as necessary to force countries to enter into fair trade agreements.

We are told that there are these non-tariff barriers. And so our response is to eliminate the only barriers we have and get killed one at a time with these non-tariff barriers as if we can change this one, and oh, they have got that one. And we only see the ones they published. Most of them are on the phone where individual companies are told not to buy American goods.

The way to deal with the non-tariff barriers is to have results or in trade agreements. Buy our stuff or don't sell in our markets. Don't think that you can benefit by playing with a procedure game and then having many of your procedures under the table. We are an open society. They can have commissars as they do in Vietnam tell their companies not to buy American goods. If American congressmen were to call companies and tell them not to buy goods we would be laughed at. Whereas, there, if there is any laughter businesses can be sent to re-education camps, business people can be sent to re-education camps.

We are told that sometimes the trade deficit is higher—well, the trade deficit keeps going up or is substantially and persistently high. That is true when we save, it is true when we fail to save. It is true when we have a budget deficit of over $1 trillion. It is true when we have a huge surplus. It is true when we have a huge surplus and are saving and our trading partners are running 3, 4, 5 percent of GDP deficits and they are not saving. The only thing that remains the same is we always have a trade deficit no matter what we do if we keep the same trade policies. One exception. If we are willing to have a calamity of the type we had in 2008, then we get to keep our same trade policies and see a reduction in the trade deficit.

I suggest that we find a different way to bring down the trade deficit. I am amazed that there is no discussion in this country of moving in a new direction. All the choice is, keep the policies that have failed or double down on the policies that have failed.

And finally, I think at least one witness suggested that huge trade deficits have nothing to do with jobs. The huge increases in imports cannot displace American workers. Ms. Drake, is it possible that huge increases in imports could adversely affect American workers?

Ms. DRAKE. It is really disingenuous to say that exports create jobs but imports have no effect on jobs. As you said, you have to look at both sides of the equation, and quite frankly our trade deficit represents the fact that we are consuming more than we produce. And that means there is an opportunity cost for lost jobs, either real jobs that we had that are gone or jobs that we could have had if we produced things here. So we really do have to look at net exports and that is the number we want to increase if we want to have good trade policy.

To the chairman's point about is there anything that is preventing companies from offshoring now? No, that is the status quo. But the danger of the TPP is that it provides additional incentives to offshore so that we actually speed it. And it can do that through the ISDS mechanism by saying to those who offshore, you now have additional influence over the rules this economy makes and if you would like to threaten it in the case that it passes a food safety law or worker protection law or you don't like the zoning decision that it made you can do that.

And we know that that is being used and it is being used for exactly those kinds of things. So what we want to make sure is that the TPP provides the right rules that actually incentivize manufacturing here. And trade can be done right. Congressman Kaptur said she supported the U.S.-Jordan Free Trade Agreement. So did the AFL–CIO. I think if we look at how Germany does trade, if we look at how Sweden does trade, they do a lot of exporting in an advanced economy and they haven't seen the extensive job losses that we have.

When you look at productivity, to Ms. Overby's point, when productivity increases workers should do better. They are contributing more, their firm is making more money, they should get a part of it. But what we have seen is a complete decoupling of worker productivity and wages. And that is not, it is in the United States but it is not just here.

And it does have to do with globalization, because if we set up rules that make it much easier for firms to say, hey, take this pay cut or we are moving, and we do that in every country, firms can game countries. Who has got the weakest environmental regulations? Who is going to pay the lowest wages? And that is not good for workers or businesses. Because in the end what businesses want are middle classes who can be consumers who can buy things. And when we have such a demand shortage here because of wage stagnation and you have it elsewhere, we have a problem exporting more goods because there aren't folks who can buy them.

And just to one last point on Fast Track and the full transparency. Again I would say be really careful, because Fast Track in the past has always been for a time period—4 years or 5 years or something like this, so trade agreements can be negotiated that weren't even thought of when the Fast Track was granted. Think about how Korea was negotiated right at the very end of President Bush's Fast Track term. That was not something that Congress had contemplated when they passed the Fast Track deal, and I would dispute that it was well negotiated. We think it was rushed. We think it left jobs on the table. And we think the extraordinarily increase in deficits that we have seen just in the first couple of years of Korea are evidence that something is really wrong with that agreement. So I think we can do better, and that is really what we are here to say.

One last thing. I don't think the question is if the TPP fails. I think the question is how to do the TPP. The U.S. has entered into trade negotiations before that have failed with Malaysia, with Thailand, with Europe a couple of times, and we still have stature. And think the question is how do we do this right? Not pull out, not cede space to China, but do things that are good for workers in China and the U.S. and that will be good for all of us.

Mr. SHERMAN. I think my time is expired.

Ms. KAPTUR. Mr. Chairman, I can't thank you enough, and the ranking member, for allowing me to be here today and to listen to the witnesses. I appreciate your collegiality.

Mr. SALMON. Thank you. I am going to just close by saying that I got this from the Korea Economic Institute of America. This is just my district not the entire country, but the Arizona Fifth District merchandise exports to Korea grew to 18.6 million. It grew 28 percent, up 25 percent from 2013. In the service sector exports grew 13.2 percent to 24.3 million from 2012, and the jobs related to trade with Korea in my district are 297.

So I understand. There is going to be other dialogue. This isn't the last hearing on TPP. We will have lots of other hearings. I really appreciate the comments. I appreciate the loyal opposition. That is the way it is supposed to be. And we appreciate the wonderful job that everybody on the panel did. And without objection——

Mr. SHERMAN. Mr. Chairman, just make them get you import statistics for your district as well so you can lay them next to each other. And with that, thank you very much.

Mr. SALMON. Thank you. This meeting is adjourned. Thank you.

[Whereupon, at 4:51 p.m., the subcommittee was adjourned.]

APPENDIX

MATERIAL SUBMITTED FOR THE RECORD

SUBCOMMITTEE HEARING NOTICE
COMMITTEE ON FOREIGN AFFAIRS
U.S. HOUSE OF REPRESENTATIVES
WASHINGTON, DC 20515-6128

Subcommittee on Asia and the Pacific
Matt Salmon (R-AZ), Chairman

March 4, 2015

TO: MEMBERS OF THE COMMITTEE ON FOREIGN AFFAIRS

You are respectfully requested to attend an OPEN hearing of the Committee on Foreign Affairs, to be held by the Subcommittee on Asia and the Pacific in Room 2172 of the Rayburn House Office Building (and available live on the Committee website at http://www.ForeignAffairs.house.gov):

DATE: Wednesday, March 4, 2015

TIME: 3:00 p.m.

SUBJECT: The Trans-Pacific Partnership: Prospects for Greater U.S. Trade

WITNESSES: Claude Barfield, Ph.D.
                   Resident Scholar
                   American Enterprise Institute

                   Ms. Tami Overby
                   Senior Vice President for Asia
                   U.S. Chamber of Commerce

                   Mr. Scott Miller
                   Senior Adviser and William M. Scholl Chair in International Business
                   Center for Strategic and International Studies

                   Ms. Celeste Drake
                   Trade and Globalization Policy Specialist
                   The American Federation of Labor and Congress of Industrial Organizations

By Direction of the Chairman

The Committee on Foreign Affairs seeks to make its facilities accessible to persons with disabilities. If you are in need of special accommodations, please call 202/225-5021 at least four business days in advance of the event, whenever practicable. Questions with regard to special accommodations in general (including availability of Committee materials in alternative formats and assistive listening devices) may be directed to the Committee.

TIME SCHEDULED TO RECONVENE _____
or
TIME ADJOURNED ___*4:51pm*___

Subcommittee Staff Director

Statement for the Record
Mr. Connolly of Virginia

As part of a broader strategic rebalance to the Asia-Pacific, the Trans-Pacific Partnership (TPP) is at the nexus of geopolitics and trade. Trade has become one of America's most powerful foreign policy tools, and the 12-nation trade talks could potentially conclude the largest U.S. free trade agreement in history.

In a continent where many of our existing relationships are defined by robust trading partnerships, a high quality TPP deal would deepen U.S. alliances and strengthen ties to emerging partners. Most important, it would do so on our terms. America would set the rules for engagement in the Asia-Pacific where we already maintain longstanding commitments.

If we hope to counter China in the Asia-Pacific, we must make a value proposition to the region. That proposition must comprise both the enduring commitment the U.S. has demonstrated to the people of the Asia-Pacific as well as a path to prosperity defined by American values.

This is not an expedition into parts unknown. We have a record. The U.S. has lasting relationships in the region where we have planted seeds of civil society, bolstered democratic gains, and promoted American values through trade. South Korea, a longtime recipient of U.S. foreign aid, became a donor of official development assistance in 1987. Korea is now a democracy of 51 million people with the world's 12th largest economy and 29th highest GDP per capita. It is also part of a strategically valuable relationship important to addressing threats on the Korean peninsula, constraining North Korea, and ultimately reunifying the peninsula under a democratic government. Our relationship with Korea is a model we should hope to emulate for our relationships in the Asia-Pacific.

Of the 11 nations with which the U.S. is currently negotiating TPP, 6 already have free trade agreements with the U.S. The TPP negotiations represent an opportunity to expand on strong economic ties our nation has to the region. The participating nations comprise 40 percent of the global economy and account for nearly one-third of global trade. This does not include potential future participants to an agreement such as Korea and Taiwan.

The geopolitical stakes could not be higher. Advancing an American-led rules-based order for the Asia-Pacific will have reverberations into every facet of our presence in the region. However, we must ensure that those reverberations are ringing endorsements of American values and norms.

Through deepened economic ties with the region, the U.S. will be well-positioned to shape trade and industry practices. The U.S should use the negotiations to insist on strong labor and environmental protections, particularly in countries where we have concerns about current standards. We cannot be satisfied with just any deal. We must have assurances that this deal is not injurious to the American worker and that it creates opportunities for the American middle class. The deal must be consistent with our values and advance our interests in the region.

QUESTION FOR THE RECORD

THE HON. TOM MARINO (PA-10)

HOUSE COMMITTEE ON FOREIGN AFFAIRS – SUBCOMMITTEE ON
ASIA AND THE PACIFIC

SUBCOMMITTEE HEARING: *THE TRANS-PACIFIC PARTNERSHIP: PROSPECTES
FOR GREATER U.S. TRADE*

MARCH 4, 2015

QUESTION OF ALL WITNESSES:
As a member of this Subcommittee and as a member of the House Judiciary Committee's
Subcommittee on Courts, Intellectual Property, and the Internet I am very interested in ensuring
that authors and inventors in the United States are able to secure exclusive rights to their writings
and discoveries – as guaranteed by the *Constitution*.

As commerce continues to migrate to the internet, I believe it becomes increasingly imperative
that trade agreements reflect our Constitutional principles by promoting the development of
legitimate e-commerce and protecting intellectual property rights online.

Can you please explain what mechanisms the Trans-Pacific Partnership agreement should
include to foster legitimate online commerce?

[NOTE: The subcommittee received no responses to the above questions prior to
printing.]